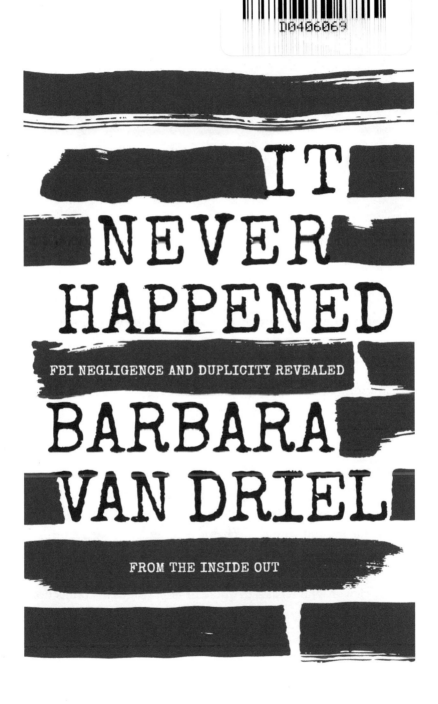

IT NEVER HAPPENED

FBI NEGLIGENCE AND DUPLICITY REVEALED

BARBARA VAN DRIEL

FROM THE INSIDE OUT

It Never Happened: FBI Negligence and Duplicity
Revealed from the Inside Out

978-1-7325394-1-9 (paperback)
978-1-7325394-0-2 (eBook)

Published by FravanLithoPress

Publishing Consultant: David Wogahn, DavidWogahn.com

For Dad

CONTENTS

ACKNOWLEDGMENTS

FIRST OFF, I want to thank the many men and women with whom I worked during my years in the FBI. Due to privacy issues, they must remain anonymous. Because of the events chronicled in this book, one might assume I did not hold people within the FBI in high regard. That is not the case. There were many individuals who embodied the admirable qualities that we all desire in our public servants. To them, I remain grateful.

In addition, many family members and friends have supported me over the years, both while I worked as a Special Agent and after my departure from the Bureau. I thank them for trying to understand the reasons I left, even though for most of them it made no sense. Sometimes those closest to you must remain in the dark.

In particular, I would like to thank Sara McLaughlin for her invaluable assistance with the first draft of this book, and my nephew, A. M. Lysy, for his inestimable work on subsequent drafts, including creative consultation and editing. Without them, this book would not be.

Lastly, thanks to Julia and Jared at Wildbound PR for their enthusiasm and insightful recommendations.

—

The names of all persons in the FBI, except Robert Hanssen and the author, have been changed in order to protect their identities. The opinions expressed in this book are solely those of the author and not the FBI.

INTRODUCTION

I WAS born to be an FBI agent.

From as far back as I can remember, my desire was to find something greater than myself, something to be devoted to. It took years to form my character and personality, but I consistently always strove for excellence in my academics and honesty in my personal dealings.

I learned my work ethic from my dad. Of Dutch and Irish descent, he worked forty-five years as a lithographer. He took pride in his craft, and his level of devotion made a tremendous impression on me. I am my father's daughter.

When I first began my college education, I studied economics, philosophy, and music. I played the piano, sang contemporary and classical songs, and composed piano music. Some of the lyrics I wrote seem corny now, but I enjoyed the challenge of writing music. I've always loved challenges.

After a brief stop out in order to earn some money for school, I transferred to a college in the Midwest and soon found what I thought I'd be truly suited to: an academic program to prepare me for a career in law. Although I quickly acclimated to my studies, I was still uncertain what my actual career path would be.

And then I met Louie Lee Barney.

He was an attorney, one of my adjunct professors, who soon became my mentor and friend. Eventually, he strongly urged me to apply to the FBI. He saw in me something that I could not see in myself. Much to my surprise, one day he took the opportunity to speak to me very seriously about my future: "You are exactly what the FBI is looking for—patriotic and honest to a fault."

I was in shock. Perhaps I could get a job as a cop … but the FBI? … right out of college? … with no previous law enforcement experience? *What*?

But I trusted Louie Lee, and if he believed that I was what the Bureau wanted, then I was going to go for it one-thousand percent. And that's what I did. I would try to realize a dream that I had first expressed at the age of seven: an older cousin asked me what I wanted to be when I grew up; leaning on the handlebars of my blue Royce Union, without hesitation I said: an FBI agent.

So, this is my story, a true story of dedication, sacrifice, fidelity, courage—and tremendous heartbreak. That's what happens to a person who truly believes and puts her all into her dream. It was a thrill, it was an honor, and it was a cruel thing.

Would I change anything? Not really. As my career unfolded, as you will see, the path became littered with abuse, deception, and tremendous pressure to compromise the ethics that I could not compromise. But I was never prepared to live a falsehood, on any level, for any person or organization, even when it cost me personally.

—

If you ever wondered what it would be like to be an FBI Special Agent, this book is for you. If you want to know what life was like for a female agent, you've come to the right place. When I joined in early 1983, I became part of a distinguished group: only about 420 women had ever been Special Agents. An honor, and a bit of a burden.

A particular psychological seduction makes one feel as if one belongs to a family. Becoming a Special Agent with the FBI had all the feel of just such a seduction, wielding a palpable power over every facet of one's life. The painful truth was that many members of this "family" could not be trusted. Why? As I came to learn, powerful bureaucracies ultimately serve themselves.

My motivation for joining the Bureau was to serve my country, but for the reasons evident in this book, I could not successfully fulfill my calling. Not only did the Bureau fail to provide crucial support but, in many cases, fellow agents actively discouraged or prevented me from doing my work. To this point, you will meet Robert Hanssen, my first supervisor in New York and the most notorious traitor in the history of the United States. You will see how the Bureau's counterintelligence culture fostered indolence, ultimately enabling him to hide his acts of espionage.

I debated over when to write this book—or even whether to write it at all. For years, friends urged me to do so, but I agonized over the decision. I waited this long because I needed time to free myself from judgments clouded by emotion. Leaving the Bureau felt like getting a divorce, and I didn't want to disparage my "spouse" out of spite.

Some of the events described in this book are so preposterous that, if they hadn't happened to me, I would have difficulty believing them. My style of writing is in the form of free-flowing "vignettes" as I attempt to capture through the totality of specific experiences the ethos of the FBI's counterintelligence culture. And I would emphasize that I am specifically referring to that work, those agents, not the agents who worked criminal cases.

However, I promise that every word is true—every incident of sexual harassment/assault, every single betrayal, every threat. They all undermined my efforts to serve. As the title of this book appropriately suggests, with respect to the career that I had hoped for as a Special Agent with the FBI—"it never happened."

CHAPTER 1

YOU'RE KILLING ME

I REMEMBER it was a blue-sky day, late August 1981.

As I walked into the small interview room on my college campus, Pittsburg State University (Pittsburg, Kansas), his piercing blue eyes caught my attention. It was obvious that Clint Matthews, the Special Agent (SA) who handled new agent recruiting in the Kansas City, Missouri Division (KCMO), was someone not to be toyed with. It was all in those eyes.

But what threw me was his nearly bald head and beige turtleneck. What was going on! My stereotypical idea of an agent made me wonder: where's the full head of hair? The starched white shirt and tie? I was reeling after only twenty seconds.

And then he spoke: "You're killing me."

My pretty pink seersucker outfit suddenly felt like a cement suit. I had merely handed him my one-page resume, and the interview was over already? I hadn't even taken a seat yet.

I later learned that his incredible skills of discernment along with his tough work ethic found him ranked number two Bureau-wide as a new agent recruiter, in spite of the fact that KCMO was one of the smaller divisions.

A moment later he looked me in the eyes and asked if I had ever broken the law.

"No." Those blue eyes were really cutting into me now.

"Well, if that's the case, you *will* be an agent."

He went on to explain that I had "ruined his day" because he had never before found even one eligible candidate in the nearly ten years he had been coming to the Pittsburg campus. What he meant was that, because I had selected the first time slot in the morning, there was no way that the rest of his day would be productive— losers and wannabees until quitting time. What was the chance of finding another candidate on the same day?

"Wow," I thought, "he sure is *direct*."

I readily admitted to Clint that I had tried pot twice— when I was sixteen. No problem. The Bureau standard regarding illegal drug use in the 80s was using marijuana fewer than five times before the age of twenty-one.

As the thirty-minute interview came to an end, Clint offered to return to campus in early October. He was willing to bring the two exams I had to take, even though those exams were not supposed to leave Division headquarters. My friends began to tease me with juvenile comments, such as "he's just trying to get in your pants."

The vetting process was quite involved: I had to prepare a thorough application that included every job I had ever had, every residence, detailed information on three acquaintances and three references of my choice, educational history, any drug use, any health issues, and a whole lot more.

When Clint brought the exams to my campus, I noted the academic exam contained two sections: antonyms and synonyms; analogies. It was intentionally designed to see whether or not a candidate could follow instructions: answer only the questions you knew, and you would do well; attempt to answer all the questions, and you were sure to flunk. No "educated guesses," thank you very much.

In the midst of the exam, I wondered to myself if even William F. Buckley, Jr. would know these words. In the analogies (A is to B as C is to D), I rarely knew more than one of the four words. I walked out of the first exam, my eyes wide as saucers.

"What's the problem?" Clint asked.

"Well, I just failed. No need to continue with the psychological exam."

"How many questions did you answer?"

"Oh, about forty to forty-five."

"*What?*"

"Yeah, I know. There were one hundred and ten questions and I only knew forty or so."

"You *knew* forty? You didn't guess? Barb, the average candidate usually only knows about twenty questions."

The psychological portion was geared to assess one's competitive attitude. Clint was not allowed to coach me in any way. He merely told me to be aggressive, very aggressive. And those blue eyes flashed.

I remember one question:

If I misplace my keys, I will
- a) absolutely find them within five minutes.
- b) find them after a thirty-minute search.
- c) come across them by accident two days later.
- d) happen upon them one month hence.
- e) never find them.

Of course, I chose "a" because it was true—until one month later when, in real life, my house keys "hid" from me in a school binder. I was mystified. I shook the binder repeatedly but no keys. One week later, they fell out of that very binder! I guess those keys just about made a liar out of me.

Oddly enough, on the same day that Clint showed up with the exams, he later made a surprise appearance somewhere else on campus. During my singing performance of "Caro Mio Bien," I spotted a familiar bald head in my line of sight. What was Clint doing there! Admittedly, I felt honored. He had gone out of his way to be supportive.

I still remember the day I received my first letter from the FBI, the results of the two exams. The magic number was "32" for women and minorities, and "35" for white males. I hated what I perceived as a double standard.

Wanting to enter the Bureau with my head held high, I had already told Clint I would not accept an appointment as Special Agent if I did not receive a "white-male score." He had argued with me, but I was adamant. I was not going to put up with any crap about getting in as an "EEO stat."

Standing in the kitchen of my basement apartment there in Pittsburg, I held the thin, long business envelope. My hands were literally shaking. Taking a deep breath, I carefully tore the edge. My eyes could barely take in the words—they scurried to locate the magic number. Was it … was it … it was: 35.12.

I had made the second cut!

In the spring of 1982, I was invited to KCMO for the "big interview": three senior FBI agents from the Division and me.

Clint greeted me warmly, trying to assure me that this interview was going to go smoothly: "The guys are great."

"Any advice?"

"No one-word answers. And if the interview ends before ninety minutes, that's bad. If it goes past the two-hour mark, you're in."

I sat down in the only empty chair in the rather large interview room. Two agents sat to my right: one close, on a diagonal to me and staring in my direction; the other, immediately to my right, looking off. The third agent, the power suit, sat behind a desk across the room. It was soon obvious that he was in charge of the interview.

The questions ranged from politics to sports to literature to personal interests and hobbies. Even philosophical ideas were on the table. I soon felt quite comfortable. The interview had subtly metamorphosed into a real conversation. And at about the one-hour mark, I noted the language had changed: the "ifs" had turned to "whens."

I was slowly entering their world. That invisible threshold was just before me. I could feel it.

The agent to my immediate right sat forward in his chair, elbows on his knees, scrutinizing me out of the corner of his eye. He never shifted position. I tried not to look at him too often as I was beginning to become unnerved by his presence.

"He must be the guy who does the profile of me," I attempted to comfort myself. The other two agents engaged me readily.

Then, the Scrutinizer finally spoke: "Are you going through this applicant process just to see if you can become an agent?"

I replied that I had only prepared one copy of my resume: I was in—all the way. But I wondered how I could convince him of my sincerity. The question implied that I was playing a game, was not serious about accepting the appointment if offered.

A whole other hour went by before he spoke again!

And he asked the same question—*verbatim*. What was with this guy?

Same answer. I felt helpless to convince him of my sincerity. Maybe it wasn't even possible.

At the two-hour mark, I didn't move. I was elated. The interview was a success!

We were all still talking—except the Scrutinizer, who had already asked his one question, twice. Strangely enough, the Power Suit had indulged himself with a protracted story of his personal struggle to quit smoking. Although it seemed a bit inappropriate for the time and place, I was able to respond in like kind by describing my father's own process of quitting. We were bonding, even if it was a bit unorthodox.

Much to my surprise, Clint later told me that the Scrutinizer had wanted to award me a perfect interview score. The Suit had taken exception to the fact that I didn't know who had won the NCAA Championship that year (boo-hoo!), so he knocked me down a couple of points in the "Range of Interests" category.

All in all, however, I received a viable score. I had made the third cut and was on "The List." Now, I just had to wait for the call when a training slot came open.

That call came the following January.

CHAPTER 2

LOVE, QUANTICO STYLE

"BARBARA, YOU'VE made a terrible mistake."

These words shot through my mind moments after we piled onto the bus at the J. Edgar Hoover Building in Washington, D.C., that was to take us to Quantico, Virginia, the site of the FBI Academy. Class 83-3 (twenty-seven of us: twenty men, seven women) was to be my family for the next sixteen weeks. But already I had this awful sinking feeling as I caught snippets of silly banter echoing inside the bus. It seemed so adolescent. Where were we heading, on a high-school class trip? Nerves, perhaps.

The day before, another new agent and I had been sworn in by the KCMO Special Agent in Charge (SAC). The ceremony was brief and private, just the three of us. The intention of the swearing in was meant to be life-altering. We were entering a world with new rules devised by an unseen hierarchy. It was already apparent that this was not a job; this was not even a career. This was going to be a 24/7 life.

My entering on duty (EOD) date was February 6, 1983, Ronald Reagan's birthday. I had President Reagan to thank for getting into the Bureau at all because under President Jimmy Carter there had been a hiring freeze. At any rate, my journey was beginning.

Our arrival at Quantico in rural Virginia was unceremonious. The job for the day was to get settled into our dorm rooms. My "quad" had just three gals: I was the seventh female, since the room assignments were based on an alphabetical arrangement. Therefore, I was all by myself on my side of the quad. The three of us shared a small bathroom between the two bedrooms.

Mia and Terese were two very nice young women. A red-head, Terese (I later nicknamed "the gazelle" because of her running style) was demure, a loner. Mia, a Latin-American goddess, was not only vivacious but also a sincere friend during my time at the Academy.

Day two at Quantico was our introduction to the Physical Education (PE) program. We had to be tested in order to establish a physical fitness baseline. Clint Matthews had strongly warned me: be prepared to run two miles at a decent pace (sixteen to eighteen minutes) and be able to do a reasonable number of sit-ups, modified pull-ups, and men's push-ups in order to stay under the radar. Points were awarded for each category, with a minimum requirement in each. The Bureau wanted to see some level of fitness at the outset. You dared not show up out of shape.

The Quantico regimen included two other aspects: academics and firearms. There were standards in each area that had to be met. Academically, all courses had to be successfully completed with no less than 85% (no "C" students here). In firearms, a 75% minimum score was required in three out of the four timed runs in order to qualify. By that I mean we ran and shot, assuming various firing positions, all on the clock.

The entire program for new agents was geared to applying the greatest amount of stress to see what could make you break. Occasionally, someone would. Depending on the situation, the event could spell the end of your time with the FBI....

My class arrives one morning at the gym for PE class, and one of our instructors—"the Maniac"—has a special game in mind for us. A deck of cards is sitting on the floor. The Maniac wants to know who would like to play cards. The game goes like this: as each card is turned over, it reveals how many push-ups or sit-ups we will be doing; aces are fifteen, face cards, ten. Assuming the push-up position, we begin. Ten of spades, ten push-ups; eight of diamonds, eight sit-ups. And back and forth we go through the entire deck.

All fifty-two cards accounted for, the Maniac smiles and wants to know if anyone is tired. He's not. So we do another deck. As we wait for each card to be turned over, we're all shaking uncontrollably from muscle fatigue. If anyone collapses to the floor while poised in the push-up position … well, you don't want to find out what will happen.

Now, the question is, who will snap? This is a game. He knows it, we know it. And he's loving every minute of it. But the Maniac has something to prove: the Bureau never quits; an agent never quits. Never.

———

Although we were not allowed to leave the Academy for the first ten weeks of training, there were a few moments where I could grab a little alone time. After twelve hours of constant activity day in and day out, a simple stroll near the main building, where the deer grazed in the evening, was a welcome respite. Total peace and quiet.

Then, one day, I was summoned to the new agents training main office for a phone call. It was Clint from Kansas City.

"What the hell's going on with you?" he asked, his voice ringing with accusation. "I've been getting reports back here that you've been seen walking alone over in the firearms area after class."

"Yeah, so what's the point?"

Silence.

I felt violated. Someone had been watching me and thought it necessary to "report me" to Clint. Why was I being watched? The idea of it unnerved me. He never did tell me who or why, but an ominous feeling stayed with me for some time.

After just a few days on campus, a new agent from another class pulled me aside to warn me: never be seen alone with the Director of Quantico. He fancied himself a real lady's man and was reputed to select a young woman from each new class to be "his girl." You'd do well to avoid that label. If lover boy passed me in the corridor—the main building was a maze of corridors—I nodded and kept going. He was dashing, to be sure, but I was not getting into any romances at Quantico. I had actually promised Clint before leaving Kansas City that I would keep my nose clean—and he had promised *me* that he'd kick my butt if he ever got word that I wasn't.

Quantico, after all, was replete with heartbreaking stories of new agents getting involved with each other. The pressure of the place fostered these tenuous attachments. They almost never ended well, and the added risk was everyone knew your business.

—

A month or so into my training, I had the happy occasion to bump into a Marine one day when I was at the gym. I always got a kick out of the Marines and their running cadence. But did it really work? He took me out for a one-mile run. He sang the entire time—believe it or not—running *backwards*, while I ran full out, grimacing outwardly yet smiling inwardly. It worked, and it was the only six-minute mile I ever ran. Because of him, I was able to shave one minute from my time on the two-mile run. And that was big!

On the other hand, the academic program was a breeze for me. Six of us in our class tied for the highest grade: 98.6%. I enjoyed my studies (except for briefing cases in law class) and assiduously applied myself.

As for firearms, well…. I never learned to enjoy firing a gun. I envied those guys who could go out and shoot 98-100%. I was lucky to get a 75%. My biggest problem: the sight picture. It never made sense to me that you had to look at the sights and not the silhouette target. Therefore, my eyes would shift quickly back and forth— sights, target, sights, target—and I would pull low or miss high. I didn't even realize I was doing this most of the time. But my scores reflected it.

The day before qualifying, we went through a dry run: sixty rounds in two and a half minutes, multiple positions, the whole drill four times. I eked out a 74.5%— once. I was dejected. That night, I sat in my room with tears in my eyes. Had I come this far to fail? It seems melodramatic now, but I actually mentally rehearsed my resignation statement: "I would like to thank President Reagan for all he's done for me, and I apologize to the American people for wasting their hard-earned money on my stay at Quantico, but as a result of my ineptitude, I just can't hit the target. Before they escort me off the field, I'm going."

As I was composing my statement, one of the two class counselors assigned to 83-3 knocked on my door around eight o'clock at night. He explained to me in great detail how I was inefficiently loading my revolver. What I was doing was removing the bullets from my side-by-side pouch two at a time, but then placing them into the cylinder *one* at a time. This inefficiency gobbled up precious seconds, causing undue stress. I was defeating myself without knowing it.

As he said goodnight, my counselor advised, "Practice with your red handle tonight and try not to worry."

A red-handle gun was issued to each new agent to allow him or her to practice alone in the dorms. The barrel of the gun was plugged, but the cylinder could be opened and loaded with dummy rounds.

Although I practiced, in my heart I felt sick. If I did not qualify tomorrow afternoon, I would have one day of remedial firearms with an instructor and one more chance to run the course. If I didn't pass then, I would be immediately escorted from the field, to the gun vault, to my room, and to the airport—all in the same afternoon. It had happened to others. The Bureau was firm on this point. No wiggle room.

That night I had a heart-to-heart talk with the Lord. And I practiced my loading technique.

With ten weeks under my belt, my day of reckoning had arrived. I was filled with anticipation. As I ran the line the first time, I had the sense that Someone else was pulling the trigger. On my way to retrieving my first target in order to score it, I looked up to my right. One of my firearms instructors was smiling ear to ear, thumbs up. He could see my target from his vantage point in the firearms tower. He knew. I had passed.

I was speechless after scoring the target: 92.5%. The next two runs went just as well: 87.5% and 93.0%. My feet did not touch the ground the rest of the afternoon. I realized I would make it. I would be an FBI agent. And I never forgot my instructor's smile and much-needed championing that day.

Despite the occasional encouragement I received from my different instructors, there was an absolute undercurrent of misogyny at Quantico. You noticed the need of some white males to lash out at the women. On more than one occasion, I defended myself with "Hey, I entered with a white-male score." The point I had made to Clint more than a year earlier was now very relevant: some of these white guys really resented the people who entered the Bureau because of EEO regs.

One new agent in our class, a real macho dude, took it upon himself to administer his own brand of "tough love." One day, we were running as a class indoors. Three abreast, nine in each column, we had to circle the gym until the instructor told us to stop. Mr. Machismo was behind me. As we jogged, I looked over my left shoulder. I caught his eye and smiled slightly.

"Fuck you!" he hissed.

I recoiled. What was *that*? Where was that animus coming from?

This was not the first time he had mouthed off to me. He would often say something snide in class, like mocking my distance-glasses. I didn't get it. Not until our last day at Quantico.

"Hey, agent, you took a lot of shit from me over the past few months. You're going to make a great agent!"

"Yeah, thanks," I replied weakly. So (condescendingly) thoughtful....

—

The day of graduation from Quantico finally arrived: May 20, 1983. Everyone in my class invited their families to attend the ceremony. Most people had one or two guests. My family went all out: thirteen of my relatives traveled to Virginia.

The day was impressive. First, a ceremony was held in which the Director of Quantico presented each agent with his or her FBI credentials, then there was a firearms demonstration featuring remarkable feats of marksmanship, primarily by the firearms instructors. My father was especially proud of my accomplishments in this area because I had never fired a gun before Quantico.

All of this was followed by an FBI-sponsored luncheon off campus. There, I introduced one of my firearms instructors, SA Ron Williams, to my family and, at my father's insistence, he was invited to sit at our table.

Following the meal, Williams volunteered to give me a ride back to Quantico to pick up my bags. He was going that way, so it was no trouble. My family was impressed that I seemed to be singled out for special treatment. I felt honored, too, because, of all my instructors, I held him in the highest regard. I was in awe of this man.

We climbed into his Camaro and chatted casually about the day's events during the fifteen-minute ride. When we arrived in the parking lot, we sat for several minutes talking in the car.

Suddenly, I felt his huge hands grab my shoulders, twist my body, and pull me close to him. His lips engulfed my face and he shoved his tongue deep inside my mouth. I went numb. Embarrassed, unable to speak, my mind reeled. I needed to get out of the car, quickly, without escalating the situation. Somehow I did.

My day ruined, this moment saw all my regard for Williams evaporate. I never had any contact with him again.

More than the graduation ceremony itself, this incident officially initiated me into the life that awaited me. Had I made a terrible mistake? I guess time would tell.

CHAPTER 3

THE SHERIFF

ON THE morning of May 25th, I arrived at the KCMO office filled with renewed enthusiasm—a real "blue flamer"—determined to put the offensive event with Williams behind me.

As I waited for Clint Matthews in the lobby, my mind raced. What squad would I be assigned to? Would the other agents like me? Would I be successful? Clint greeted me with a firm handshake and smile. His attitude seemed different. He silently communicated that we were now peers: the kid was all grown up.

As we serpentined our way through the corridors, I noticed the place was large and bland: old tile floors, bare walls (I can't remember any color), numerous squad rooms with randomly placed poles (ostensibly holding up the ceiling, one would assume). A bit unimpressive.

Clint's small office was located adjacent to the squad supervisor's and within the Background Investigations/

Civil Rights Matters (BI/CRM) squad area. Entering, we each took a seat, he behind his desk, I across from him.

"I've got good news for you," he said. "SA Barney Appleton, a fine Christian man, is going to be your training agent on the Criminal Matters squad."

New agents were assigned to work with a senior agent for the first thirty to sixty days in their first office of assignment. This practice was a way of bridging the chasm between Quantico and the "real world." Frankly, the prerequisites for becoming a training agent in the field were never explained to me. In short order, however, I realized that one simply had to be alive and breathing in order to qualify.

After some perfunctory niceties in Clint's office, Appleton showed me to my desk in our squad room a couple of doors down. He made it a regular practice to volunteer to train new agents coming out of Quantico. Appleton advised me to look through the files stacked there, as they were the cases/leads assigned to me. As I sat there, I took note of Appleton's appearance: tall, dark-haired, middle-aged, wearing cowboy boots and a big western-buckled belt, with the stereotypical pot belly pushing on the middle buttons of his shirt. He sat about fifteen feet off to my left, diagonally. The squad room— aka "the bullpen"—had about twelve desks arranged in groupings of four. Everything was out in the open, as they say.

Looking over my files that morning, little did I know that Appleton had a "baptism by fire" planned for my first day. He was taking me along on one of his Unlawful Flight to Avoid Prosecution (UFAP) investigations.

We arrived at a Kansas City, Kansas, apartment complex around midday. As it turned out, the subject was nowhere to be found, but his girlfriend was in the apartment. Sitting on a sofa in the living room, she cried openly as Appleton verbally bullied her. She was scared to death and appeared not to know where her boyfriend was. When Appleton backed off a bit, I took the opportunity to quietly say a few words of comfort to her. She was not a suspect or subject; she was an innocent person in the wrong place at the wrong time. And the bullying had achieved nothing except to make her more upset.

Moments later, Appleton pulled me into the hallway.

"If you want to be nice to people, go become a social worker."

He was angry that I had spoken to this woman with kindness. Why? Was I showing weakness? Was I being "girly"? No. He was just angry. But, wait, Clint had said he was such a good Christian man.

Back in the Bureau car, Appleton's annoyance was palpable. As he peered over his aviator-shaped sunglasses, his arrogance was on full display. With no witnesses, of course, Appleton laid into me about resigning from the FBI.

"Do yourself, and the Bureau, a favor and resign today."

I was flabbergasted. And I did not attempt to defend myself.

With these words my first day working as a Special Agent came to an end. Could a first day have ended any more bizarrely?

—

Over the next sixty days, Appleton made it his mission to break my spirit, finding fault with anything and everything I did. What I soon discovered, however, was he volunteered to be a training agent because no one wanted to work with him. This way he had control over at least one other person on the squad on a quite regular basis. Other agents would sometimes stop by my desk and talk with me, offering condolences because I was forced to work with "the Sheriff."

Once, when we were riding in his Bureau car, he lectured me on the role of women in society, using his Baptist wife as the ultimate role model.

"My wife stays home with our children and realizes she has no contribution to make in the world of men, especially in law enforcement. What is it going to take for me to convince you that your place in life is as a wife and mother?"

Appleton fancied himself an authority on everything, especially writing up cases. After I prepared a handwritten rough draft of an interview that I was going to submit to the typing pool, Appleton demanded, as usual, to review it. As I stood beside his desk, he grabbed his pen and hastily scribbled in red ink across the whole of the first page, "This is unproffesional." Certainly he meant *unprofessional*, but I dared not say a word. After all, he was the consummate authority on everything, which must have included spelling.

Those same words were echoed a few months later by another new agent in training. This red-haired, obviously bright journalism major laughed as he told me how Appleton had pooh-poohed his paperwork. "Can you believe it?" he asked.

Appleton even made me go study some of his closed files in order to educate myself in the ways of a real agent—him. In one criminal case report, Appleton had documented some sexual activity. According to the master, two men could perform cunnilingus on each other, and two women, fellatio. I laughed until I cried.

I really did want to cry because this swaggering misogynist seemed to hold the future of my career in his hands.

I was never quite sure whether I was the target of an office prank or whether Appleton was (or both of us), but, one day, someone wallpapered the pillars in our squad room with pictures of two androgynous bodies intertwined. Superimposed on their faces were actual photos of our own. The practical joker or jokers remained anonymous, although the mockery hung in the air. Here I was, a month into my "career," the only woman on the squad, and I was being subjected to harassment as well as humiliation. No one defended me, no one objected.

What really bothered me was the audacity required to pull off this stunt. One or more agents had accessed my personnel file in order to lift my photo. And much to my disbelief, the supervisor was mum; he didn't even have the images taken down.

At the end of the two-month training period with Appleton, he recommended that I be reassigned. I gladly moved to the BI/CRM squad. My new boss, Supervisory Special Agent (SSA) Mark Donaldson, immediately picked up on my discouragement. He quickly let it be known that he loved working with women and was happy to have me on his squad. And he reassured me that, as far as all the nonsense that had gone on with Appleton, that was over. He was confident that I could handle any assignment. Regardless of what Appleton had said, the word on the street was, "Barbara can do paper." This expression referred to a high level of competence when writing reports.

I flourished under Donaldson's supervision and was grateful to now be on a squad where I was respected. The four months I spent there would be the first and last time I ever enjoyed a period of genuine camaraderie while in the Bureau.

CHAPTER 4

HOUSTON, WE HAVE
A PROBLEM

AFTER SIX months in Kansas City, according to then-Bureau policy, I was officially transferred to my next assignment, the Houston Division. This was my introduction to the counterintelligence (CI) world.

A couple of days after arriving on the squad, SA Kip Tucker approached me. I wasn't seated at my desk because I didn't have one. I was playing "musical desks," working out of a brown cardboard box until a permanent spot became available. He wondered if I would be interested in working with him. My first question was "Do I get a desk?" Then I thought, maybe he and I could be partners! I jumped at the opportunity.

One of the first things my would-be partner had me do was spend a couple of minutes with a senior agent on the Asian Matters squad (located in the same space as the Soviet Matters squad). He had something *real* important to show me.

As I walked up to the guy, he barely acknowledged my presence. I indicated that Tucker had sent me over to get some *true* Bureau wisdom from him, sage advice if you will. Immediately, a spark lit, cherubs sang, he was in his groove.

"This is—*the*—*most*—*important*—thing I do every day."

He pointed to his calendar covered with black Xs that marked his countdown to retirement. He was persevering—only five years, three months, and two weeks left. This was hard work counting down *so* many days. But, come on, somebody had to do it.

I reeled back in disgust. This was how a senior CI agent viewed his career. Total boredom. His attitude made me sick: he was clearly staying on for the job security and pension, nothing else.

Unfortunately, he wasn't alone. Many agents spent a lot of time going to the gym, the mall, doing their personal business on Bureau time. This meant more to them than doing what they were paid to do. Sometimes agents called the office and asked other agents for a favor: to be signed in or signed out. I didn't know there was such a thing as "phoning it in" when your job was Special Agent in counterintelligence.

I had only been an agent for six months, but already my rose-colored glasses were being knocked off. Looking back, this squad was par for the course in terms of waste, apathy, and negligence. I had a lot to learn.

———

Right away, Tucker and I started our little routine: morning coffee for Tucker, the boss (SSA Anthony Navarro), the squad secretary, and me. I walked downstairs each morning to get coffee and bring it back. While we drank it, Tucker and I set out our leads for the day. Two or three for me, the same for him.

Not long after joining the squad, Tucker needed to discuss a serious problem with me. It concerned the squad's Number One Register. That term referred to the sign-in sheet for the squad.

"The other agents are having a fit because you're signing in at the actual time you arrive at the office."

"So ... and the problem is?"

"Um. You need to sign in a minute or two after the last person has signed in."

"I have a problem with that."

"And that is?"

"It's not the truth."

Silence. Consternation. I had the feeling that Tucker had never run into a person like me before, and he had been an agent for nearly twenty-three years.

We resolved the problem by agreeing that I would sign in after every other agent on the squad. That way, since everyone else pretended to arrive between six and six-twenty in the morning, my arrival time, which was usually close to eight, could be recorded last. The books needed to be accurate after all.

This noble tradition of "banging the book" or fudging one's arrival time to the office grew out of the requirement for each agent to put in overtime to the tune of one hundred and ten minutes per day on average. This administratively unaccountable overtime—"AUO," as it was called—was well compensated. Ironically, what began as a built-in bonus, became an opportunity to abuse the system.

—

We had a real cast of characters on our CI squad, which handled Soviet and other non-Asian Matters. I couldn't believe it when, one day, my supervisor called me into his office to ask me if I would be willing to help another agent out with some of his cases.

SA Jay Fox had arrived in Houston just after me as he was in Class 83-4, right behind my class at Quantico. I began to pay attention to Fox's daily routine. After all, I was now carrying his water and wanted to know why he couldn't get his cases done. Each morning, he arrived with briefcase and gym bag in hand. I can still see him sitting at his desk, fussing over the two pieces of paper in front of him, playing with his colored pushpins. He had three colors: green for cases completed, yellow for pending cases, and red for untouched cases. I noted that most of the pins on his board were red.

But what really got to me was that every day Fox stood up at exactly twelve noon, picked up his gym bag, and left the office. He didn't even try to conceal the fact that he was heading for the gym. He would usually return about four-thirty, having spent nearly four hours goofing off, at the gym, whatever. He was a loner, usually spoke to no one, and really hated his job. That much was obvious from his demeanor.

Fox told me one day—the rare time he lowered himself to speak to someone on our squad—how he had been an airline pilot, and that it was the most *boring* job on earth. I laughed a couple of years later when I learned that he had resigned from the Bureau and gone back to working as a pilot. Wow!

By the way, in addition to handling my own thirty cases or so, I completed more than twenty of Fox's in less than one month. They were no sweat—a breeze, in fact—but evidently Fox didn't understand working by the sweat of the brow. He preferred lifting weights and picking up that hefty paycheck every other Thursday.

———

SA Mort Farley nearly defies description. Anytime he arrived at the office, regardless of the time, he looked as if he had just gotten home from a hard day's work—his knotted tie pulled to one side with the top shirt button undone. He drove the lemon of the squad, a beat-up Pinto, and basically hid out most of the time. He was the king of "sign me in, sign me out." But he would have everyone believe he was out there saving America from all known evil.

After Farley had procrastinated for nearly six months to get a lead done that was highly pertinent to a case of mine, I had had it. I went to see Navarro.

"I know Farley needs to get that lead done on your case, Barb, but he's kinda busy."

"Boss, he's had only *one* lead assigned to him for the past six months. Why can't he get it done? I need that lead covered."

"Uh … now, uh … let's see if we can work around the situation."

"Okay. Why not just give me the lead?"

"I can't appear to be reprimanding Farley."

"Why not? Ugh. Well … okay. Then let's tell him that we know he's really busy right now, so we'll handle this lead for him. This way we won't hurt his feelings."

Navarro breathed a sigh of relief.

—

Basic CI cases were opened for 120 days. That is, the case agent had four months to complete the investigation. I would normally turn these cases over in two to three weeks. But soon after beginning on the squad, I realized I was working too hard for some of those around me.

Tucker sat me down one day to go over the rules of the road. One-hundred-and-twenty-day cases needed to be nursed along: put one piece of paper in the file on day 118, and then request an extension. A one-hundred-and-twenty-day extension would be automatically granted. This really rubbed me wrong—just one more example of corrupting the system.

On rare occasions a case might require extra time to complete. But as a regular practice? I could never bring myself to do it. And I was slowly learning that Tucker was not the ideal role model for me.

———

Arrogance was not limited to Special Agents alone. One Investigative Assistant (IA) reeked of it. Unfortunately, he was a necessary evil in the life of an agent. The IA was responsible for certain basic documentation that was part of a case. There was no getting around it.

With this one particular IA, you were not to speak until he looked up from his desk and silently acknowledged your presence. He might be talking on the phone, filing his nails (literally!), shuffling papers. No matter. You were not to interrupt him. And you didn't dare cross him, I was warned: your request form would mysteriously disappear, deposited in the nearest trashcan. I did my best to avoid this individual. Unaccustomed to kissing butt, I had to really bite my tongue in his presence.

———

A big CI surveillance case came up unexpectedly. Numerous agents and the Special Surveillance Group (SSG), a non-agent surveillance team, were dispatched to another city in Texas about two hours away. We would be gone for a couple of days.

I left Houston with SA Tim Saunders, a thin, quiet man, who enjoyed running and homemade brew. His running regimen was of colossal proportions as he was permanently in training for twenty-four-hour, quarter-mile-track marathons. By his own admission, Saunders didn't have much of a life besides running.

About thirty minutes outside of Houston, I heard Fox's voice come over the Bureau radio. At first, I didn't realize what was going on. There was a lot of garbled talk. Then it hit me: some of the agents were playing Trivial Pursuit, and Fox was trying to coax us into joining in. I refused to pick up the hand receiver. Saunders laughed; he could care less.

We arrived at our destination mid-afternoon. Saunders had already broached the topic of beer: did I imbibe? He had a case of homemade cold ones in the trunk of our Bucar. As my mind raced—I had heard the frequent admonition "broads, Bucars, and beer don't mix" often enough—I realized he wasn't kidding. He pulled the car over and parked under the shade of a tree. The team of agents gathered around as Saunders popped open beer after beer and passed out the brown, unlabelled bottles.

I couldn't believe it. I wasn't interested in joining in, and my unwillingness to participate soon found me relegated to the motel room where the tech guy was set up. Some lame excuse was given about needing an agent inside to document the surveillance, but I knew the guys wanted to get rid of me. I wasn't a team player; I didn't know how to have fun.

In the room, the top tech guru from FBI Headquarters explained all the equipment to me, told me about his long and very successful career as an electronic surveillance specialist, and really put me at ease. He was a super guy.

About one in the morning, my tech-mate said good night. I would be alone in the room till about six, but not to worry: the subjects were tucked in bed, sound asleep, and two agents were on foot outside, just in case.

A loud knock on my door a couple of hours later startled me into consciousness. I shot up out of bed and looked through the peephole. SAs Mike and Ike were at my door. They wanted in. These two jerks were supposed to be watching the subjects' room from a remote location—and here they were trying to get in my room!

More banging on the door. Against my better judgment, I finally let them in. Both staggered through the doorway—drunk. My brief career flashed before me: the potential for this to jeopardize the operation was very real. Despite my protests they absolutely refused to leave. As I climbed back into bed, covering myself with the blanket and bedspread, I watched the two of them slowly slide down the wall, sinking to the floor. Within moments, they had passed out.

The next day, we packed up and returned to Houston. The ride back with Saunders was tense, quiet. I was furious.

I was called into the SAC's office the following morning. His Assistant Special Agent in Charge (ASAC) began to interrogate me. And that's exactly what it was: an interrogation. He wanted to know what had gone on during the surveillance—specifically, in the motel room.

But, wait, there were *three* of us in the motel room. Where were Mike and Ike *now*?

I thought to myself, "Do I tell the truth—become a snitch? Or might it be best to minimize the situation?" I decided the truth was my best and only option. The ASAC wasn't happy and angrily informed me at the end of the interrogation that I was lucky I had told the truth. He already knew what had happened, and I would have been in big trouble if I had lied. Ludicrous.

Mike was an obvious alcoholic; his sidekick, Ike, had just gone along with him that night. But nothing was done to either agent, and no one cared to help Mike with his alcohol problem. I later asked Tucker about the guy, but he told me to mind my own business. Although Mike was an accident waiting to happen, the powers-that-be turned a blind eye to the situation.

Status quo, as usual.

CHAPTER 5

THE REAL FAKE ARM

THE LAST thing I expected to see on a CIA officer was an artificial hand.

Grace Stevens entered our CI squad space with a lavender trench coat draped over her right arm. Tucker and I quietly escorted her into SSA Navarro's office in order to have a detailed conversation about our pending meeting with a civilian.

As we were concluding, Stevens reached down into her purse on the floor to grab a pen. It was then that I noticed she was wearing a fixed prosthetic hand. Momentarily startled—as I was dumbstruck that Tucker had not mentioned this to me following his three-hour luncheon with her several weeks earlier—I tried to silently signal him with my eyes. It may have been a small matter, but I was slightly beside myself because my repeated attempts to get his attention fell flat. Tucker was oblivious.

"Hey, Kip, why don't you and I ride together and meet Grace there?"

"Nah, you go with her and I'll meet you."

"Uh, well, wouldn't it be better if we rode together in order to discuss a bit more of our strategy?"

"No, not necessary. You ride with Grace."

I reluctantly left the office with Stevens.

We rendezvoused with the civilian at a neighboring upscale Greek restaurant. The young woman nervously shifted in her seat as we approached. She was intimidated, no doubt. I introduced her to Grace. We were there in hopes that this private citizen would be willing to become a "friend of the Bureau" (and the Agency).

Forty minutes or so into the conversation, and with two beers under his belt, Tucker suddenly went slack: the revelation had hit him between the eyes. He was in a near-panic. He quickly moved to have the meeting come to an end.

Grace, the civilian, and I left first. Tucker paid the bill. The gals and I said our goodbyes, and I waited in the parking lot for Tucker.

With the bright sunlight blinding me, I could barely see him rushing up to me.

"What's with the disguise?" he bellowed.

"What disguise?"

"That fake arm!"

"Kip, that's a *real* fake arm. I tried to signal you in Tony's office, but you ignored my cues. You just insisted that I ride with Grace. How could I possibly let you know?"

It seemed that the beers had heightened his awareness but dulled his critical thinking ability, since he assumed the CIA officer had donned a fake arm for this special occasion.

What a preposterous idea! Here was a senior agent with tens of thousands of hours of investigative experience asking such a question. A *disguise*? I was speechless.

CHAPTER 6

QUANTICO REVISITED

RETURNING TO Quantico for a four-day in-service, nearly a year after graduating from new agents training, I looked forward to seeing an acquaintance of mine, the agent who was second in command at the Academy. During my new agents training, he had gone out of his way to be supportive of me, especially during PE class, and every so often I would drop by his office to say hello. Since leaving Quantico, I had loosely kept in touch—one or two telephone calls.

I considered him a mentor and had looked forward to maintaining a career-long professional relationship. Upon my arrival, I stopped by his office for a visit. It was great to see each other again. He was the same good guy I remembered.

After catching up for a few minutes, we agreed to go to dinner on my last night at Quantico. Italian. He'd drive.

On the way to the restaurant, the conversation covered the highlights of the past year. He seemed genuinely interested. We couldn't stop laughing about the jerks we mutually knew at Quantico. It'd been so long since I'd had such a good laugh.

At dinner, however, after consuming a carafe of red wine, my acquaintance sloppily steered the conversation from our mutual Bureau experiences to his unhappy marriage. Uh-oh. My thoughts abruptly returned to the criticism I had endured a year ago. I had defended him before my former suite-mates, Mia and Terese, arguing that he was a genuine good guy. I still believed in the possibility of the archetypical platonic friendship. They, however, had warned me I was wrong about him: he had ulterior motives.

Suddenly slobbering, he awkwardly put his arm around my shoulder and pulled me in close. His demeanor shifted from friendly to overtly sexual. The implication couldn't be missed, and I knew that whatever "friendship" I thought was possible was never going to happen.

Using my best diplomatic skills, I deftly extricated myself from his grasp, and our dinner came to an end. We rode back to Quantico in silence.

That night he officially fell off his pedestal. And after that evening, we never spoke again.

On the flight back to Houston, I reflected on the life I was living as this "big-shot" FBI agent. Where was it all heading? With just about one year in the field, I was already successfully handling my cases, but I was slowly realizing the esprit de corps of the Bureau was nothing more than an illusion.

CHAPTER 7

STEPPING DOWN

COFFEE DRINKERS do what it takes to get their fix.

I loved the daily four-flight trek to bring coffee back for my supervisor, my partner, my secretary, and myself when I worked in the Houston office.

There was an agent who occasionally graced our squad with his presence when he wasn't off on assignment on account of his bilingual skills, English/Spanish. Hector Osorio loved to brag about these special gigs. He would wave his Bureau-issued checks in front of us so as to underscore his "premier" position. I barely knew the guy, but, one day, for some reason he seemed quite friendly toward me.

He indicated he'd like to tag along for the morning coffee run. I explained that I didn't sit around yucking it up in the coffee shop. My routine was to come directly back to the squad after picking up the drinks.

I headed for the door at the far end of our squad room. Osorio decided to join me.

The two of us were simply walking down the stairs, talking about nothing in particular, when, as I stepped onto the landing between flights, out of nowhere Osorio grabbed me, spun me around, and slammed his body against mine. His erect penis pressed against me as he forcefully thrust his tongue down my throat.

I shoved him away with both hands and bolted back up the two flights of stairs. My heart raced, my mind was numb.

The next thing I knew I was walking straight toward my supervisor's empty office, where Kip Tucker stood just outside the door (he was "sitting the desk" that day since Navarro was out).

"Get in here—right now," I said firmly, without breaking my stride.

He followed me in and shut the door.

"You're not going to believe what Hector just did."

I calmly told him what happened despite the quaking emotions that nearly got the best of me.

"Drop it," Tucker said coldly. "If you take this any further, you'll be destroyed."

I couldn't believe what I was hearing. My partner was telling me that what had occurred did not matter. All I wanted was an opportunity to file a complaint with our EEO officer. Ironically, that was Navarro.

"How about if we both are polygraphed? I'm willing to do that to prove I'm telling the truth," I said as a last-ditch effort to get him to act in my behalf.

Tucker's position was intransigent. He forbade me to take the matter any further. In essence, he ordered me to shut up and pretend it never happened. The worst part of this experience was the realization that if I reported anything not in keeping with the Bureau's implicit convention, I would be shunned. I had a growing feeling that any danger that would befall me, particularly at the hands of my fellow agents, would never be addressed appropriately. For the first time, I didn't feel safe. And I was without recourse.

There weren't many female agents, so, apparently, Osorio assumed he had the right to grope anyone without recrimination. As it turned out, he had good instincts.

CHAPTER 8

THE EX-MONK

AGENTS BECOME quickly accustomed to being treated like royalty, from being individually escorted onto airplanes to jumping the line at the bank anytime they flash their creds.

I knew agents had to be assertive if not at times downright aggressive. I was no fool. There was room for all kinds: oddballs, pencil-pushers, status-seekers, gentlemen. However, I'm not sure even the Bureau was big enough for more than one guy like Kip Tucker.

A senior agent, Tucker was a former monk. A "devout" Catholic, he was married with five children. My "rites of initiation" were handled by Tucker, who offered to train me in the subtleties of CI investigations. As the proverbial "new kid on the block," it was important that I understood the rules of the road.

Tucker told me about two *mandatory* rites of passage: sharing a beer (wrapped in a brown-paper bag) in a Bucar; attending a movie matinee with one's partner.

It sounded goofy, but what did I know? After all, Tucker was my partner and seemed to be going out of his way to teach me. Many months later, close to the end of my time in Houston, I finally acquiesced to his persistent reminders. We'd do the matinee.

While we sat in the darkened theater watching *Amadeus* one late Friday afternoon, Mozart wasn't the only one making overtures. Like some hormone-crazed teenager, Tucker kept touching me, despite my repeated attempts to pull away.

I remember how strange and subtle he acted, scooching over every so often against the armrest until he was nearly in my lap. He was also pulling me toward him.

When the lights finally came up, I decided to ignore his inappropriate behavior. He didn't say anything, so I wasn't going to. He acted like nothing had happened as we rode back to the office in his Bucar. Not a word.

However, nothing prepared me for the day, two weeks later, when Tucker barged into my apartment, pinned me down on my bed, and shouted: "I won't take no for an answer!"

It was our practice for Tucker to occasionally drop me off at the back door of my apartment so I could eat lunch. I remember one Friday, in early November, he dropped me off about noon. When he came back to pick me up an hour later, he tapped lightly on the back door. I opened it. I turned my back to pick my purse up off the bed, and Tucker was on me. He made an attempt to embrace me. I resisted. At that point, he grabbed me by both wrists and wrestled me toward the bed. In a moment, I was pinned down. He was literally on top of me.

"What're you *doing*? Get off me!" I tried to snap him back into reality: "You're a married man with five children."

"I don't care. I'll worry about that tomorrow."

"No you won't. We'll worry about it right now."

He finally went limp. Without a word, he slid off the bed and left.

Me? I was inconsolable. Any good feelings from the previous ten months working with him had just been wiped out. A partner? He was no partner of mine. He was a predator. Now I had a little insight as to why he had, in essence, defended Osorio back in April. Birds of a feather fucking flocked together.

The next morning, we had a scheduled meeting with an Army officer who was involved in one of my cases. After an hour and a half, the officer asked me, "What's going on here? Why aren't you guys talking to each other?"

"Ask him," I replied.

Tucker ignored him.

When Monday came, I called in sick. Tuesday, did the same. Tucker had the audacity to come by my apartment about one in the afternoon. Cracking the door slightly with the security chain latched, I said, "I don't want to talk to you," and slammed the door.

On Wednesday, I finally had to go back to work, but I decided it was best to keep away from him for a while.

No more partnering on cases, no more morning coffees. We kept our distance for the next month or so, avoiding the obvious.

Right before I departed for foreign language school in late December, Tucker dealt his final blow. He was obviously trying to be cruel.

"I used to watch you put your left hand on the seat when we rode in the car, and I thought you wanted me to hold it."

"What? No way. I wasn't consciously doing anything."

"Well, you were the one constantly talking. I was just listening."

"I thought we were friends. That's what friends do. They talk."

"You're the one that needed a friend—not me."

Really, I was the one who "needed a friend"? Frankly, I was learning, real fast, that friendship and trust were in short supply in the FBI.

CHAPTER 9

RUSSIAN INTERLUDE

MY APTITUDE score in foreign languages was high enough that I was given four choices: Korean, Chinese, Arabic, or Russian. It didn't take me long to figure out Chinese men prefer working with men; Arabic is read right to left with too many squiggly dots above and below the lines. Korean—no clue. What kind of caseload would I have? I was a Reagan girl; I went with the language of the former "Evil Empire."

Only two people volunteered when the Bureau-wide memo went around looking for agents who wanted to study Russian at the Defense Language Institute (DLI) in Monterey, California. The target date: New Year's Day, 1985.

I packed up my apartment and drove my '81 Dodge Colt from Houston to California. In Monterey, I found a one-bedroom apartment within walking distance from campus. The town was gorgeous, and I was excited about my new assignment—full-time school. It felt good to hang up my investigative boots for the foreseeable future, as I wanted to put the unfortunate incidents of the past year behind me. It was a much-needed break from my Bureau "compadres."

Between ninety and one hundred military personnel were enrolled in the Basic Russian course. I was the sole civilian. All four branches of the Armed Services were represented. We hit the ground running, as it was early on explained to us that two weeks in class were the equivalent of one semester in college. More than a week of missed classes meant starting over or being dismissed.

Upon arrival, my supervisor in the Monterey office told me I needed to keep at least a 94% overall grade in order to remain at DLI or I would be sent back to my field office (with my tail between my legs). That thought was overwhelming. The potential humiliation. The overall attrition rate was nearly 50%, even though my classmates needed only a 70% average to stay in the school.

The eight-to-four regimen, plus five hours of homework, Sunday through Thursday without exception, was beyond grueling. By April, I was reconsidering my commitment. Was this worth it?

I contacted my supervisory agent and asked for a face-to-face meeting. I told him I wanted out of the program and was seriously considering resigning from the Bureau. To his credit, my supervisor presented me with a challenge: "Think about it for two weeks, and if after that time you still want to leave, I'll support your decision."

That permission to speak my mind without recrimination was refreshing. I am certain he never let on to my field office (Houston) that I was contemplating quitting the language program and resigning. This supervisor had my back and had given me really good counsel.

After a couple of weeks, I felt better and never considered quitting again. As I applied myself to my studies, I learned to appreciate the beauty of the Russian language with its elegant complexity—six cases, five verb tenses.

Classes went smoothly until August when the "Lamp-Post Lady," as a few of us affectionately referred to our homeroom teacher, suddenly announced she was going to the Soviet Union to see her elderly father. She would be gone at least a month, maybe longer, so our section would be split up. Instructor Valentin Savchuk was my favorite teacher, so I requested to be put into his section and managed to be placed there after some diplomatic dialoguing with the headmistress.

Savchuk was a wonderful teacher, and, over the course of the next few months, became a close friend of mine, even confiding in me that he suffered from depression. He once commented that he was so happy to be an American, having left Ukraine more than thirty-five years earlier. He told me his greatest happiness was that he had taught me the Russian language so I could serve our country. He felt like family to me. I told him that, when I left DLI, I planned to take him back east where he could live with my father. He had no one. Unfortunately, on February 1, 1986, my dear friend died in his sleep.

I graduated the basic course with a 94%. Because I did so well, I was allowed to go on to Intermediate Russian, completing that course eight months later with a 97%. Then, after finishing a short third course in mid-October, I received the Alexander Pushkin Award for Excellence. As an independent student that second year, I flourished.

One of my potential second-year tutors was a divorced man in his mid-fifties and of Russian descent. After a brief discussion in his office, he invited me to come to his home for tutoring the following day after class.

Upon arriving, I noticed this instructor was in the kitchen preparing supper. He asked me if I would like to have a bite to eat. Then I noticed that the apartment was so small that the sitting area/work area was his bedroom. We moved into the bedroom to sit on the edge of his bed with our food. Apprehensive but still not alarmed, I took out my books.

With a thick Russian accent, he blurted out, "I noticed that your skin is broken-out." I'm sure I looked embarrassed. All of a sudden, I was self-conscious.

As it turned out, however, this was my lucky day: he had a ready solution.

"I can give you my semen to spread on your face if you'd like."

Was he deranged? He was serious. Inside, I froze. But I immediately made some excuse to leave and got the hell out of there, never to return. So much for "free" tutoring.

Oh well … just another day in the exciting life of an FBI agent.

CHAPTER 10

THE JOGGER, THE COWBOY, AND THE SCAMP

JUST IMAGINE working on the infamous SSA Robert Philip Hanssen's counterintelligence squad at a Bureau off-site location in Manhattan. I spent nearly two years in this dysfunctional office, a veritable circus. Hanssen never wanted to be disturbed and stayed in his office, with the door closed, typing away incessantly on his computer. The behavior seemed odd. Of course, in retrospect, I now know that Hanssen, aka "Ramon" to the Soviets, was betraying his country under our noses.

Hanssen's right-hand man, SA Kevin Knox, met me at Penn Station when I arrived my first day on the job in New York City. Six feet tall, Knox had wavy blonde hair and a runner's physique. As we walked to the office, he took it upon himself to give me the lay of the land.

"The first carpool departs every afternoon at one."

He wasn't kidding. Agents in New York were notoriously lazy. When I worked elsewhere, I had been told never to send a lead to New York City because it wouldn't get covered. Now I knew why. As Knox explained to me on that forty-five-minute walk, he arrived at our office each morning at about seven-thirty and left by eight for Central Park where he ran a jogging club. Usually back by noon, he stayed an hour or so, did a little paperwork, read some pages of a paperback novel, and went home.

In the office, oddly enough, Knox became annoyed watching me generate reports. Shortly after my arrival on the squad, he, with his feet propped up on his desk, pointed at the nearby oversized garbage can and said, "You see that? You might as well stop writing those reports because that's where they're going."

Not only with Knox, but across the board, working at even an average pace was discouraged on my squad. Based on his statement, I now understood that my production level could call into question what others on the squad were or were not doing (or had or had not done in the past). Another lesson in maintaining the status quo.

———

Two months after I joined the squad, Knox had to run interference between the scamp, SA Mandy Boltar, and me. She wasn't doing her work, which meant I couldn't do mine. After repeated attempts to convince Boltar to get it done, I told Knox I was going to talk to Hanssen.

Knox flipped: "Under no circumstances are you to go to Bob with any problems on the squad."

I was perplexed. I tried to reason with myself as to why the squad was being run this way. The modus operandi was deflection, not resolution. There was a method to Bob's madness, we were just in the dark about it.

Boltar and I eventually worked things out, and she started warming up to me. She told me about herself, where she was from, and about her two daughters. She wanted to promote their modeling careers, especially the older one. They were approximately ten and twelve. Boltar arranged her work schedule with their careers as her top priority. She went so far as to bring them to our secure site, where they would sit in the reception area until mommy was ready to take them for their glamour shots. They were Shirley Temples, waiting to be discovered, until the day Boltar ended it all: "Those gay make-up artists put their dirty spit all over the lipstick brushes, and I'm afraid they're going to give my girls a disease." Boltar dramatically licked her imaginary brush, puckered her lips, and pretended she was applying lipstick on someone to demonstrate her disgust with homosexual cosmetologists. Such *savoir faire*!

Ironically, Boltar had no qualms about compromising national security, traipsing in and out of the undercover site with her rug rats. She was a clueless dumb blonde but expert at banging the book, competent in every manipulation possible, from calling in six hours after her shift started to be signed in, to calling in at three in the afternoon to inform us that she wasn't coming in at all for the day shift. She expected whoever answered the phone to be her personal secretary. Basically, she worked ten hours a week—except those weeks she only worked five.

I remember the time she bounded into the office, carrying on about following some weirdo on foot on her way to work. She said, "I almost had to pull my gun on him because I was sure he was up to something."

"*What?*"

Annoyed, she replied, "I don't wanna get into it." She just wanted me to be impressed and added, "Luckily, some cops were nearby, and they handled the situation." That's all we needed—an FBI agent pulling her weapon on the streets of Manhattan on an innocent bystander she imagined to be a spy.

When Boltar got "promoted" off our squad, she landed on a downtown one where she obviously continued her antics. Within a month, alarming calls were coming in: "Who *is* this woman? She claims she regularly catches spies committing acts of espionage on the streets of Manhattan. How are we going to get rid of her? We're going to have to transfer her."

Typical Bureau fashion—pass the problem off instead of confronting it. Only the innocent are confronted.

—

The first time I ever laid eyes on SA Cole Landon, he was strutting through the office, carrying a brown lunch bag, with an I-dare-you-to-speak-to-me look on his face.

His light gray cowboy hat, blue jeans, and high-gloss-polished brown cowboy boots completed the image. I whispered to my associate, "Who is *that*?"

"That's Cole Landon, and if you know what's good for you, you'll have nothing to do with him."

I was taken aback by my colleague's statement. "Why?"

"He's a bit mentally disturbed. Before joining the Bureau, he was a Navy Seal, and now he's suing the government because they won't let him join the Naval Reserve," my associate added.

"But why the arrogant attitude?" I asked.

"He's allowed to come and go as he pleases. And after he settles in and has dinner, you just watch: he's going to pick up his gym bag and leave the office, and he won't be back until after midnight."

"Where does he go?"

"No one knows."

Peculiar, I thought, and decided to take my colleague's advice and avoid Landon. For one thing, I normally worked the day shift, and Landon's usual schedule was two back-to-back shifts (four to midnight/midnight to eight).

He would come in—never at four, maybe five, maybe six-thirty—eat his dinner, hang around the office for an hour or so, look at the papers on his desk, and then leave around seven, seven-thirty for the gym.

One morning at about two, three of us were working—not including Landon, who was out on one of his jaunts. Somewhat alarmed, Boltar suddenly appeared in my doorway.

"Cole's on the phone. He wants someone to sign him out. What should I do?"

"I don't know," I replied. "Do what you want but don't get me involved." Remember, I had been warned.

About an hour and a half later, Boltar reappeared, this time with another agent, and they both were agitated.

"Cole's on the phone again. He says he's not coming back to the office, and he's demanding one of us sign him out."

"What's the matter with him? Why can't he come back to the office?" I asked.

"He's hurt."

Coincidentally, just that morning, another agent on our squad had relayed to me two equally bizarre incidents from Landon's past. On one occasion, he had not been able to come back to the office late one night, and when he showed up the next day, he had a black eye and was missing a front tooth. His explanation? He had dropped a barbell on his face.

More alarming, a year or so earlier, this same agent, along with Assistant Supervisor Knox, had been drawn down on in the office in the middle of the night. Why? Because Landon claimed they had startled him—an absurd idea, given the fact that the space was secure. The only people who could access the front door beyond the reception area were employees of the FBI assigned to the squad. This outrageous behavior resulted in no disciplinary action.

Under no circumstances did I want to have anything to do with signing Landon out at the end of the midnight shift. So we agreed no one would sign him out. Cowards that they were, Boltar and the other agent left the office about six-thirty in the morning in order to avoid Hanssen.

About an hour later, having arrived and checked the Number One Register, Hanssen confronted me.

"Where's Cole?" he asked. "Why didn't he sign out?"

"All I know is that he called at about two in the morning, and again at three-thirty, and asked to be signed out because he couldn't make it back to the office."

Hanssen seemed annoyed. He ordered me to stay, even though my shift was over, and to document what had occurred overnight. With those words, he went back to his office. I intentionally did nothing because I had learned while in Houston the great government maxim: "A job put off is a job half done."

About an hour later, Landon showed up and walked directly into Hanssen's office, closing the door behind him. He was in there for about thirty minutes. When Landon emerged, he smugly grinned at me and left the site.

A few minutes later, Hanssen was at my doorway again.

"Forget what happened. There's no need to document anything."

I was incredulous. What was going on? First Hanssen's irritated, then he's kowtowed. What power did Landon wield over Bob?

—

About a week later, I was working a back-to-back shift. I noticed Landon's routine had changed. He stayed in the office more.

About midnight, I was minding my own business when I realized Landon had taken his gun out of its holster and placed it on top of his desk. With his back to me, he was no more than three feet away.

Landon sat there methodically cleaning his gun, almost stroking it. Then he stood up, turned around, positioned himself directly over me, and, mimicking a pistol with his right hand, pointed his index finger at my head.

"I never want to see you again as long as I live."

I was scared for my life. This guy was dead serious, and I wasn't certain how far he would take this.

I got up to go find the other agent who was working that night. She had stepped out of our small office to take a break. Unbeknownst to me, Landon had earlier threatened her, too.

Fortunately, within ten minutes, Landon was gone.

I waited around for Hanssen to arrive that morning in order to report how Landon had threatened me. Hanssen's solution was simple: take a look at the weekly schedule and only work the back-to-back shifts where Landon has not scheduled himself to be in the office.

"If by chance Cole shows up," Hanssen added, "you're to leave immediately, and you'll be paid for two days' work."

Excuse me, where was the outrage? I had been *threatened* by Landon, and Bob's "solution" was to simply work around him? His lack of concern had me incensed. More deflection.

Several times, that's just what happened: Landon would show up unexpectedly; I'd simply put my papers away and sign out. Hanssen full-well knew that Landon was playing a game, showing up willy-nilly whenever he felt like it, thereby forcing me to leave.

A couple of people on the squad subsequently told me the reason Landon had carte blanche with Hanssen: he had gone into Hanssen's unclassified garbage and found classified documents. He had Bob by the short hairs.

"Cole keeps book on Bob" was the word on the squad.

CHAPTER 11

THE MORTICIAN

EVERYONE ON the squad knew SSA Robert Hanssen was an absentee supervisor.

Bob was a computer geek. Most agents who even used computers back then did so for word processing; in the 80s, it was still customary to use cassette dictation or handwritten drafts, which would then be sent to the typing pool and turned into reports.

If you went by his office (and he rarely invited anyone in), Bob's door was closed ninety percent of the time. Odd behavior for a supervisor. When his door was open, you would see Bob, fingers flying over the computer keys, while he slouched back in his chair with his belly hung over the keyboard. No one had a clue what he was doing on that computer. The sense was there wasn't much for the squad supervisor to do.

Hanssen came and went a lot, supposedly downtown to headquarters. Our off-site squad had such a specific task that there was little need for him—or anyone, for that matter—to leave the premises in order to get casework done. So his whereabouts at any time were questionable.

My first direct contact with Hanssen was memorable: menacingly odd and slightly sexual. I was working at my desk, when he stepped out of his office, walked over and, like the proverbial spider, sat down beside me on a milk crate. Leaning forward with his legs spread wide, and without any introduction, he whispered, "You should get out of the Bureau, get married, and have a family."

Totally weird, totally scary. And then he just got up and walked back to his office.

His blatant discouragement of my ambition was particularly shocking as I had just completed twenty-one months of Russian education and was required, according to FBI regulations, to remain in the Bureau until October 1990—four years from the date of my DLI graduation. In a way, I can honestly say I never looked to have any association with him again. I felt disappointed, confused, and somewhat concerned for my well-being.

Except for the incident involving Landon, I was only alone with Hanssen on one other occasion. We were both leaving the office. He was heading to the garage; I was on my way to Penn Station.

Spontaneously, Hanssen offered, "You know, I don't have to work for a living. I'm independently wealthy."

"What the…," I thought, "Why's he telling me this?"

His statement was stunning in that I had conducted numerous background investigations, as well as counterintelligence ones, in which people who didn't have to work for a living were considered security risks—potentially vulnerable to sexual or financial seduction by enemy states.

Based on his demeanor when he said this to me, I felt he was lying. I asked another agent if she knew about this, and she said that Hanssen had bragged about his financial independence to a lot of people on the squad. Was he a confidence-seeker or a narcissistic braggart? Perhaps both.

That same agent, at one time, had worked as the Relief Supervisor. She said there was no way to convey to headquarters downtown whether anything was amiss or seemed peculiar. Headquarters made it clear: they had no use for whistleblowers.

After being on the squad for a couple of months, I had an uneasy feeling that Hanssen promoted security infractions: wanton banging of the book; his Relief Supervisor's directive to "do no work"; the underutilization of personnel; the failure to report faulty security equipment.

For example, Hanssen was in charge of making sure security protocols were in place. One day, a non-agent employee on the squad, who had devoted eighteen years to the Bureau, confided in me that she had decided to take a six-month leave of absence for mental health reasons. She explained she had been forced for a couple of years (and by the way, I'd seen this situation with my own eyes) to sit at her desk for eight hours a day, pretending that she was working when, in fact, as a result of circumstances beyond her control, she could not do her job. Due to the nature of her position, I am not at liberty to say what she did specifically for our operation. What I can say is this exemplary employee was ruined by the pressure put on her by the absurd situation.

Following her extended leave, this woman returned to the squad. With tears in her eyes, she told me, "I can't do it. I can't come back. I'm resigning."

I personally blamed Bob Hanssen for her mental breakdown. He should have helped her by preventing the problem. It took fifteen years for me to somewhat understand why things were the way they were on our squad. I'm certain now he thought that her inability to do her work was an asset in his life of deception.

———

One of the goofiest agents I met in the course of my time in the Bureau was a slacker from the South, one of the most nondescript individuals I've ever met. He had once resigned from the Bureau but had been reinstated. In New York, he definitely had reached the apex of his career—a sad fact. For all intents and purposes, his job was tantamount to loading and unloading toilet tissue rolls into those newfangled Swedish double-roll, opaque holders.

One day, he unabashedly described to me what he considered his ultimate motivation for returning to the

FBI as a Special Agent. His face glowed as he gushed over the red-carpet treatment he received every time he visited his small hometown. The Chief of Police always turned on the sirens and lights when he picked him up at the local airport, and then paraded him royally through the streets. He was an FBI agent, and that fact was all that mattered to him. I do believe I saw a glimmer of sadness in his eyes as he recounted the story of his career because he knew his life was predicated on a lie.

He added, "Even though I've never accomplished anything of value in my career, these people think I'm an American hero, and that's all that matters to me." He undoubtedly knew he would be spending the rest of his time in the Bureau on this squad. I wondered why the Bureau assigned a GS-13 to do this perfunctory task when an inexperienced clerk could have sufficed, not withstanding the national security aspect of the work on the squad. What a waste!

———

Hanssen was promoted some time in mid-1987. It was customary for supervisors to be rotated out, so he was transferred from the New York Division and replaced by a new supervisor, SSA Calvin Brainerd. Hanssen went to FBI Headquarters in Washington, D.C., on special assignment, for all we knew probably utilizing his computer expertise. We now know in retrospect he used his time in New York wisely, training himself in the use of spy paraphernalia, such as dead drops. He learned to master encoded correspondence with the Soviets, he made friends with our country's enemies—a despicably ironic allocation of a senior FBI agent's talents and resources. The most significant traitor in the history of the U.S. government had hidden his unspeakably dirty deeds and his double life right under our noses. The Bureau culture lulled us into a spirit of complacency. If you see something—mind your own fucking business.

CHAPTER 12

IRONY OF SUSPICION

WHILE WORKING in New York, as part of my ongoing education following DLI, I received Russian tutoring at a private language company, something akin to Berlitz. The one-on-one sessions were ridiculous. My immigrant tutor would read her newspaper while I read aloud my dry-bones lessons. Occasionally, she would lower her paper and mumble "dah." The Bureau paid $50 an hour, three hours a week, so I could keep my language skills fresh. What I needed her for was conversational Russian; what I got was a poor version of a Russian conversation with myself.

As summer approached, she informed me she'd be on extended vacation and her ex-husband would cover her lessons. They'd been in the United States ten years and were U.S. citizens. Ivan Durak was buoyant, enthusiastic. Now my lessons became interesting, unlike the ones taught by his ex who was obviously only working for the money.

One day, Durak suggested another student from my squad and I join him on an excursion to Brighton Beach. That town had become a small Russian community. The day of the outing, my colleague canceled, so just the two of us went. As the day progressed, his manner subtly shifted. I was getting the impression that his feelings were becoming romantic.

Within a couple of weeks, he'd asked me out; I was interested and accepted. A man on a mission, after just a couple of dates, Durak impetuously announced he had marriage intentions for our relationship. Even though he was an American citizen, I decided to go speak to my supervisor. I was concerned that the relationship might raise a red flag with the Bureau.

With this in mind, I knocked on Brainerd's door and asked if we could have a serious conversation. Until this time, my interaction with Brainerd had been minimal. His managerial position was "play the game, and take your paycheck every other week."

"My Russian instructor at the language school has asked me out, and I'm wondering if the Bureau would object if I dated him. He's pretty serious, even talking marriage."

"Why would the Bureau care about that? The Bureau doesn't care about your personal life."

"He's from the Soviet Union, but he's an American citizen and has been here ten years. Wouldn't he need some additional security clearance?"

"What's his name?"

"Ivan Durak."

The Bureau required any future spouse of an employee to pass a background investigation, so I felt the Bureau would care about any risks associated with this liaison. I kept pressing the point. Because Brainerd knew Durak was my language teacher, it would have been easy to have him checked out. About a week later, Brainerd let me know there was no problem. He was emphatic that there was no issue with my pursuing the relationship.

However, by December, after just two months of dating, I had decided Durak and I were not going to be an item. End of story.

By late February, I had decided to submit my resignation for unrelated personal reasons: I felt I needed considerable time to resolve a personal relationship of great importance to me.

Two weeks after I submitted my notice, Brainerd came to my office and placed a small yellow sticky note on my desk, said nothing, and walked out. I picked up the sticky note and saw a five-figure dollar amount: $32K and change.

I immediately went to his office and confronted him.

"That's the amount of money you owe the Bureau if you leave April 1st," he said.

He couldn't tell me how he arrived at that figure, although he claimed FBI Headquarters had given him that information. Theoretically, this amount was based on my debt for my Russian schooling. I would need to write a check for that amount in order to resign.

Brainerd picked up my resignation statement: "Do you wanna tear this up, or should I?"

Fear overcame me in an instinctively childlike manner.

"Tear it up," I sighed.

He ripped it in two, and smiled.

Several months later, I learned that that figure was a lie. The actual amount I owed in order to resign was $16K and change, which I had in my retirement fund. By then, I had come under suspicion that I had been compromised professionally, and my security clearance was restricted. This action stemmed from my association with Durak. The Bureau had come to believe I was attempting to resign to cover up some security infraction.

At that point, I desperately wanted to leave the Bureau, but I thought it best not to resign under such a cloud of suspicion. My safest bet was to resolve the security issue. If I left the Bureau under suspicion, the problem would be magnified. It was the *leaving* that looked suspicious. Had I not attempted to leave, this bogus accusation would never have materialized. By the way, when I had initially given my thirty-day notice in early March, Brainerd had repeatedly inquired, "Why are you resigning?" I recall that he was not satisfied with my answer. I sensed I could not convince him of the truth: it was strictly personal, and I did not want to talk about it.

For several months, I remained under this limited status while the Bureau obviously determined how it was going to resolve the issue. In late July, FBI

Headquarters informed me that I would be going down to Washington, D.C., for an interview (interrogation) and to be polygraphed.

I was sick at heart. I knew then that I would never trust Brainerd again no matter how long I remained on his squad. This action I took as a personal vendetta by Brainerd who, as you recall, had assured me the previous October that my association with Durak was irrelevant and benign.

A close friend attempted to convince me to walk away: "You do not have to answer to them." But, you see, "fear" was the operative word. This is how the Bureau functioned. I was valuable property, and the Bureau wasn't going to let me go readily.

In August, the Bureau flew me to Washington, D.C., where I met Q, who, as he informed me, was "the number-one polygrapher in the Bureau." This curly salt-and-pepper-haired agent, who was soft spoken, invited me into an interrogation room. He explained he would conduct a detailed, protracted interview. The goal was to prepare me for the polygraph to follow.

We spent at least three hours discussing all aspects of my personal and professional life. The point was that I must be familiar with everything he would ask during the polygraph exam because only "yes" and "no" were permissible responses. He assured me there would be no surprises. As he walked me through the process he was pleasant and professional. He ultimately wanted to know whether or not Durak had ever asked me to supply him with classified materials. Of course, he had not.

Just like in the movies, I was strapped into a chair, my pointer fingers were connected to electrodes, and, similarly, other electrodes were affixed to my body. I recall that I intentionally counseled myself to respond "yes" or "no" with a monotone voice, knowing my excitable nature.

I resolved to relax, lower my blood pressure and pulse, and allow the truth to speak for itself. However, I had had enough conversations with attorneys and other agents to doubt the veracity of polygraph results. The test is operator-dependent.

"Is your name Barbara Van Driel?" he began.

I listened to the needle on the paper every time I responded. The questions went in an order. The needle never varied. I had to sit through twenty grueling questions in order to answer the big three:

"Has anyone attempted to bribe you?"

"Have you ever revealed classified information to any unauthorized individuals?"

"Have you had any unauthorized contact with enemies of the U.S. government?"

At the conclusion of the exam, my benign polygrapher excused himself for several minutes and took the results with him. When he came back, he removed his horn-rimmed glasses and said, "You passed the polygraph," and smiled. "You're fortunate you passed," he continued. "Had you not, you would have surrendered your weapon and credentials and been escorted away."

I was back in their good graces: I had satisfied their security concerns. But they had only amplified mine. I would never feel the same way about the Bureau again.

CHAPTER 13

NOT ON MY WATCH

THE GRAND irony was that while the Bureau treated me as a suspect and wasted time and money on the trip to D.C. and a polygraph, Bob Hanssen's misdeeds went unnoticed.

Within two weeks of this humiliation, it was a brave new world for Special Agent Van Driel. Word spread quickly on the squad that personnel were needed for a new assignment in the Salt Lake City Division. Starting at the end of August, two language specialists (agent or non-agent) were going to be rotated through there for a thirty-day temporary duty (TDY) assignment.

Squeals of pain erupted as these New Yorkers considered the possibility of being away from the Big Apple. New Yorkers turned up their noses at working in Utah unless they happened to love skiing. Sensing an opportunity, I quickly offered to take the first rotation out if I could go for sixty days. There were no arguments.

Despite rumors to the contrary, I was a team player, and getting on a new team was maybe just what I needed.

Temporary duty could be a lucrative adventure and a lot of fun. When an agent was assigned to the New York Division, she normally worked there at least ten years before getting her Office of Preference (OP) transfer, so I was concerned staying in New York might become a prison sentence. I'd never been to Utah. The opportunity to get in on the ground floor on a brand new major case was alluring. I wanted to go and stay as long as possible.

When the other New York female agent and I arrived at the Salt Lake City airport, SA Caleb Stout picked us up in his Bureau car. As we departed the airport, he explained the general street layout. The Mormon Temple Square marked the epicenter of the city from which all streets were laid out on a grid.

"Oh," my compatriot moaned, "this is very confusing. I think I'm going to have a real problem getting around town. I'll need a map."

"No, it's really not difficult," Stout protested.

"I totally don't get it," she whimpered.

He looked at me and rolled his eyes. I was embarrassed. The white males did occasionally have an argument.

The new assignment was in-office with a skeleton crew of permanent staff. I quickly picked up on the routine and enjoyed the challenge.

As it turned out, my literal "team-playing" in a game of pick-up basketball at a local gym landed me at a doctor's office for emergency medical care. I had chipped a bone in my right foot. The physician said he would only treat me if I stayed from beginning to end, for the duration of the treatment, approximately two months. He wanted to put a cast on the foot. He advised that my other choice was to fly immediately back to New York and have a cast put on there.

Salt Lake City SAC Barry Thompson made the call: "It isn't happening on my watch." My stay was extended for ninety days because he did not want me to leave his division injured.

My initial sixty-day assignment ultimately morphed into an eleven-month stay, followed by a permanent transfer. Thompson's vote of confidence resonated with me, his keeping me under his care meant a lot.

He'd been the ASAC in 1983 in my first office. Barry was nurturing, a really good guy. In fact, nearly all of the supervisory agents I worked under were exceptional individuals. The one or two bad eggs I dismissed as the standard deviation. Based on both my predilection and experience, I preferred being closely associated with those in authority. I was no brown-noser, but I understood the rules of being successful. I was brought up that way—respect the position if not the man.

The average agent had tremendous disdain for management, and on more than one occasion, I heard someone say, "You know how someone is selected to become a supervisor—he raises his hand."

There were two maxims all good agents followed: never go into management and never volunteer for anything. Of course, I always volunteered for everything. And if anything, Utah was a volunteer's paradise.

CHAPTER 14

PAPER GAMES

"BANGING THE book" was my introduction to Bureau paper games. Agents allowed themselves to be ethically compromised by participation in a corrupt "tradition." It was the rare agent who stood apart, signed in and out accurately, and put in his AUO.

As an agent's life in the Bureau progressed, he was slowly introduced to the "ways of paper," whether it was a travel voucher, a TDY voucher, a surveillance log, whatever. Once, a clerk from FBI Headquarters called and asked me where my TDY voucher was for one of the months I was in Utah. She asked for my total expenditures that should have been documented by receipts in case they were ever needed.

"I threw them away," I said. "I don't know what I spent at the supermarket or McDonald's last month. Just put nothing."

"What?" she exclaimed. "In all my years in the Bureau, I've never heard of an agent willing to forfeit money on a voucher just because he wanted to be honest."

There had been a misunderstanding. I'd been told I didn't need receipts because, while some vouchers required documentation, other vouchers were based on a standard per diem. Now I was being told to use my receipts to calculate the total spent each day for my living expenses.

I joked with her, "What should I do?"

She was speechless.

Finally, she said, "You're going to have to get a blank voucher, and type across it, 'I, SA Barbara Van Driel, do willingly agree to claim zero dollars for the month of March.'"

Most agents seemed to go out of their way to profit from vouchers. For example, I was tutored by the master of vouchers, Kip Tucker, in Houston. He "suggested" I always put the highest possible amount allowed for breakfast, lunch, and dinner. Breakfast might cost $6.42 for eggs, bacon, toast, and coffee; however, if the maximum allowable amount was $10.00, my tutor said to claim $9.99 if no receipt was required.

Irony upon irony, agents told me to never cheat on vouchers because you'd be fired if you were ever caught. Yet, what they did was cheat routinely, all the time, in small amounts.

My father often cautioned me on ethical matters with admonitions, such as "If your pinky's in the water, are you wet?" and "Cheat in a small thing, cheat in a big thing." I took his words to heart, thusly, these relatively small infractions were cumulatively discouraging, as not participating put me off the "team," and yet there was nothing I could do to change the system. Where was the Integrity in FBI?

The paper trails were never ending and oftentimes inaccurate. On Background Investigations, many agents used a template. They turned in virtually identical wording, no matter whom they interviewed:

"John Doe advised that applicant is an upstanding American citizen of good character and does not abuse alcohol. He fully recommends the applicant without reservation."

I wrote my reports in such a way that each stood on its own and was not laden with what is known as "bureauese." For instance, I quoted people when they made negative comments about the person I was doing a background check on.

Once, this doctoral candidate applied to become an agent. His field was genetics/molecular biology—a brilliant man, thirty-four years old, and pushing the normal maximum age of entrance, which was thirty-five. Under certain circumstances, however, the age limit could be extended to thirty-seven.

After I handled the mandatory references (people listed on his application), I went to his campus to verify his educational history. I stopped by the Biology Department in which he had spent the previous five to seven years. One professor, who had worked with him, made bug eyes when I mentioned the candidate.

"Sir, we have a way to ensure your anonymity. This individual will not be able to discover that you spoke to the FBI," I advised.

The professor seemed comforted but still wary, as he said, "In my opinion, he's mentally unstable, and I'd be afraid if he were allowed to carry a weapon."

"Why do you say that? What has he done?"

"Over the course of several years that I've been associated with this student, we've gone to dinner and the usual faculty parties with him and his wife, and he's been cordial. However, once he was informed that his work was substandard and we would not be awarding him a doctorate, he turned on us with such hostility that we became concerned, even a bit frightened."

I asked if there was someone else with whom I could speak, someone who had worked with the candidate. The second professor with whom I spoke echoed the exact same sentiments. I also knew from the candidate's application that, at the age of fifteen, his brother had murdered the family next door—parents and two children. I'm willing to bet that, if this case had landed on a fellow agent's desk, this applicant would have made it in because his application information was pristine. After all, according to his references he was a wonderful guy. Who knows? He might have made the front page—and I don't mean for stem-cell research.

Hoover used to encourage agents to go beyond the margins of the paper when doing investigations. He thought we should dig for the truth, and that's how I worked my cases. When it comes to hiring people to work not only for the FBI but also for the Department of Defense or the White House, the vetting process must be as thorough as possible. No stones should be left unturned.

—

When I was in the Salt Lake City office, after having spent many months on special assignment there, one day a voice announced over the PA system:

"SA Barbara Van Driel, please report to the SAC's office."

My first thought was something was wrong, I was in trouble. After several years in the Bureau, I'd learned that, generally speaking, it wasn't good news to be called into the big boss's office. And it was totally uncool for street agents to be seen with upper management.

As I walked into SAC Thompson's office, he stood up and greeted me.

"Take a seat," Thompson said, pointing to the leather chair behind his large mahogany desk. I thought he was kidding.

"No, thanks, that's okay."

He insisted, even though there was another chair and couch in the room. Simultaneously, he plopped down on the couch and let out a long sigh. As I moved to the beige chair in front of his desk, I noted my SAC's slack posture.

Looking despondent, Thompson said, "I need to talk to you about something."

I felt queasy, uneasy, and a bit panicked: I had so much regard for the man, I feared I had unwittingly committed some infraction. Remember, my polygraph experience back at FBI Headquarters had served to put me in a permanent state of insecurity and fear when dealing with anyone in authority. That was the Bureau way.

"I need you to be honest with me," he went on, "I am surrounded by 'yes' men and can't depend on the information I'm getting from the people around me."

When he said that to me, although I was still cautious, he somewhat allayed my fears. I'd known him since my first assignment in Kansas City, and his reputation was that of a straight shooter, a stellar individual.

"My question is this: what's going on in the undercover assignment? I have the sense that it's all paper." He sincerely wanted my opinion, and, in that sense, took me into his confidence.

I prefaced my response with one request: "If I say anything right now, I'm asking that it not leave this room."

He assured me our conversation was for his ears only. I suspected he might be baiting me, so I hesitated with a direct response. I knew exactly what the problem was, but was I certain he wanted to hear it?

I leaned toward him, looked him in the eye, and said, "If you really want the truth, I'll tell you, but you're not going to like it."

Thompson was insistent: "You've seen all the baloney in New York. I need to know if that's what's going on here."

With that remark, I dropped my defenses.

"Boss, you're creating another New York—a paper palace."

I elaborated on my comments by explaining the day-in, day-out situation in the backroom office. He seemed impressed by my candor and thanked me profusely.

Soon afterwards, my squad supervisor, SSA John Barrett, called me in to discuss my future assignment. He explained that the case I'd been working on in the office was being expanded. Undercover positions were being created.

"For a couple of these positions, your expertise is required," he told me.

I was flattered and taken aback. He handed me several sheets of paper stapled together. As I skimmed through them, I noticed five or six names on each page along with personal identifying information. This was a list of eligible candidates with a background in the Russian language.

"Do you know your rating?" Barrett asked.

"No." I didn't even know a list like this existed, let alone that I was on it.

"Well, I've looked at that list, and you're the second highest of the women. We want to offer you a permanent transfer to the Salt Lake City Division."

I was stunned. *No one* asks your permission to have you transfer to another field office. The needs of the Bureau are paramount.

I was privy to some of the office politics, but as far as his treatment of me was concerned, Barrett was fair-minded and principled. Unlike any supervisor I'd ever seen, he was at his desk morning, noon, and night. He was an expert at paper ... the good kind. And I thought he would be a fabulous boss.

Enthusiastically, I responded, "You bet!"

CHAPTER 15

GOING AWOL

"WITH THAT promise from Salt Lake City and ten cents, you can buy yourself a cup of coffee," said Homer Larsen, my ASAC in New York, with bitter sarcasm.

Let me digress.

Having the offer to permanently move to Salt Lake City, I packed my truck in Utah for the drive back to New York. I had been advised by SSA Barrett to go back to New York and wait for my official transfer papers from FBI Headquarters.

While I was driving cross-country with my father, who had flown to Salt Lake City to accompany me, I made it a point to keep in touch with my field division in New York. On day three of my seven-day trek, I called in from a phone booth in the middle of Kansas, and was put on hold. In fact, I was told by the clerk who answered that the ASAC wanted to speak with me. Odd....

Well, as soon as he got on the phone, immediately he started shouting.

"Where the hell are you? What're you doing? You weren't supposed to leave Salt Lake!"

I was thrown off balance. I didn't know where his anger was coming from.

My father, standing outside the phone booth, could see something was wrong. I tried to explain to Larsen why I was traveling back east. He yelled that I'd left without permission.

"What do you mean? My supervisor in Salt Lake *told* me to go back to New York!"

What I didn't realize was there was a turf war going on between the two divisions, Salt Lake and New York. In Larsen's opinion, *he* should be telling me when to come back to New York. It was *his* role to supervise my travel and any transfer arrangements.

I kept insisting, "I'm only doing what I was told to do." His irrational thinking frightened me. No one travels from one division to another without permission. It's not possible because a travel voucher is matched to the authorization for travel at FBI Headquarters.

"As far as I'm concerned, you're AWOL," Larsen spat. "Now, you get your ass back here."

When Larsen accused me of going AWOL, I flipped. I was absolutely beside myself. I slammed down the receiver and shouted, "You fucking asshole!"

"I can't believe you spoke that way," my father exclaimed.

And it was true. In all my life, I had never talked like this. This time, though, I had been pushed to my limit. I was so beyond exasperated by the lack of communication between the two divisions—and by the fact that I was being vilified on account of it. To be treated like a rogue agent when I was dutifully carrying out my assignment.

Absolutely preposterous.

CHAPTER 16

MORMON TABERNACLED BUREAU

WHILE ASAC Homer Larsen screamed at me for not staying in Salt Lake City, at the same time, he ordered me to "get my ass" back to New York.

As it turned out, his prophesy about ten cents and the promise of a transfer was completely inaccurate. Now, face to face in the New York Division headquarters, Larsen poured on the insults:

"Who do you think you are—a prima donna? There's no way you're going to Salt Lake City, so get back up to your squad and get used to the idea that you're staying in New York."

Four days later, a subdued Larsen called up to my squad and advised me, "You've been transferred to Salt Lake City." He saved face by intimating he had "negotiated" the transfer with FBI Headquarters.

In honor of a person's transfer, it was always a tradition that a luncheon or dinner be held. Unfortunately, many people on my squad resented me, and to add insult to injury, a couple of months after I began my TDY assignment in Salt Lake City, the much fought-for cost of living allowance (COLA) was implemented in New York City. Because I was technically "on the books" in New York (that's where my paycheck was generated), I received both TDY pay and the COLA, even though I had only worked four days in New York. An agent was always paid based on his official office of assignment until permanently transferred. The COLA amounted to a 25% increase in pay, which I received for eight months.

Clerks who were a GS-5 or GS-6 level only received a 10–15% COLA, whereas agents received the 25% COLA. This disparity created tremendous animosity between agent and non-agent personnel, adding to the contentious atmosphere already in place in New York.

When the COLA came into effect, some clerical employees went so far as to place a notice on their desks: "My COLA is less than your COLA: do it yourself." I suggested the COLA percentages be reversed because the support staff in Manhattan needed every penny they could get. My fellow agents were incensed at the suggestion, skipped my fifteen-minute farewell get-together, but did chip in for my black and white New York City skyline coffee mug. I got all choked up as I thought about what I would be missing—the good ol' days in New York. Right....

—

Ironically, Salt Lake City was both better and worse. I was confronted with a level of personal corruption I had not encountered before. Salt Lake City was replete with unique problems stemming from the distinctive Bureau culture in that office. The Mormon complement, around 50%, made life difficult for non-Mormon personnel. There was a continuous undercurrent of nepotistic action, as well as outright proselytizing.

For example, one agent, a Mormon bishop, attempted to interfere with a clerical employee's personal life. I met her as she exited the room in which he had bullied her about her fiancé. In his opinion, she needed to marry a Mormon, and he strongly encouraged her to call off her wedding. As I came upon her, she was crying hysterically. This kind of blurring the boundaries between personal and professional business was common in Salt Lake City. To underscore the concern the Bureau had, there was a policy in place at the time that forbade any Mormon to serve as the Salt Lake City Division SAC or ASAC.

Mormon agents were often doing church business on Bureau time. That is, when they weren't running their private businesses. Personal business included such things as running a construction firm or placing bets on the phone with bookies. This particular Mormon bishop had a "perfect marriage": he was both an absentee construction company owner and an absentee FBI agent—with church business thrown in for good measure.

One day, the ASAC's secretary confronted me: "What are you doing wearing that necklace?"

I looked down and said, "What's the problem with my necklace?"

She scowled and shut up.

The small gold crucifix that I was wearing was a personal affront to her. Imagine that. It wasn't as if I had a swastika tattooed on my forehead, but, based on her behavior, you would have thought so.

Even worse, one time I was conducting a Background Investigation on a potential clerical employee, and a supervisor who happened to know the young man personally from church, attempted to influence the results of my investigation. He not-so-subtly tried to discourage me from including unflattering facts that had come to light about the applicant. Like so many in that office, his perfect Bureau world would have consisted of nothing but Mormons. And he obviously had no problem compromising basic ethical norms to achieve that end.

No matter how hard I tried, the bullshit kept coming at me.

CHAPTER 17

THROUGH THE LOOKING GLASS

"DUMB IT down."

Incredibly, my contact agent's advice as I began my new undercover assignment could be summed up in those three words. You would expect highly complex and detailed training to be central to the formation of an undercover agent. In this case, I was to fly by the seat of my pants. My cover job required minimal gray matter. To come across too brainy would have caused me to come under suspicion.

Several months after I started my fake job, working as a near-minimum wage employee, I had the occasion to be alone for a few minutes with a coworker, a young woman. We jumped in a van, Melissa behind the wheel, with me riding shotgun.

Suddenly, she turned to me and blurted out, "You're not going to believe what people are saying about you."

"What?" I answered with a feeling of disconcertion.

"They believe you're an FBI agent just posing as one of us."

Thinking quickly in order to have a reasonable reaction, I chose my words carefully. If I had in any way revealed my true identity, it would have been a major catastrophe because Melissa was a blabbermouth. My cover would've been blown.

Bubbling with enthusiasm, I turned the situation around: "Do you mean the FBI is involved in this operation? Could we possibly get jobs with the FBI?"

Melissa exclaimed, "I wonder if we could!"

"I'm sure we could get a lot more money for doing this stuff if we agreed to help them out," I enthused. "Why don't you try to find out how we could work for the FBI."

The ramifications of a blown cover would be far-reaching: the start-up cost and thousands of man-hours—let alone the national security implications, and how about my career? I was expected to be able to handle curve balls. That dumb-it-down training sure came in handy that afternoon.

—

Working undercover caused me to be isolated. Combined with this was the unrelenting pressure to maintain my false identity. My day-to-day life took place just south of Salt Lake City in a quiet suburb. The sense of living in an emotional vacuum was compounded by an occasional hostile encounter with a coworker.

One of the major queen-pins, Alice, took an instant dislike to me. In most cases, our assigned jobs did not overlap, but she seemed to take some delight in marginalizing me whenever she got the opportunity. On one such occasion, I came to work in the afternoon and was told by her that I would specifically not be included on the detail the next morning, a field trip of sorts.

That evening, around midnight, I angrily spoke to my contact agent, Paul Lofton, on the phone: "That woman keeps interfering with my work, Paul."

Pissed off, he said, "This is going to come to an end. I'll take care of it and get back to you." He hung up.

The interesting thing is the FBI had intentionally not cut her in on the undercover facet of my assignment. Her position would normally have warranted it, but she was considered a security risk—she wouldn't be able to keep her mouth shut was the general opinion.

At two in the morning, Lofton called me back and advised, "Report to work at seven in the morning."

"What about Alice? She'll be really ticked off."

"Don't worry about her. We've gone over her head. Frankly, she's not in charge of anything. She just thinks she is."

Lofton evidently performed quite a magic trick, pulling this rabbit out of a hat, and in the middle of the night no less.

When I arrived, it was obvious Alice had been informed about the personnel change involving me. She glared at me from behind her gold-rimmed spectacles and said nothing. Our group piled in the vehicle and took off for the destination. More silence.

It was embarrassing when we arrived and she introduced everyone except me to our hosts. We stood in a semi-circle. She went down the line, saying each person's name, skipping me as if I were invisible.

All day, she refused to acknowledge me whatsoever, which only underscored her pettiness. I knew she would no longer be a problem because her boss had evidently told her to leave me alone. I was the lowest on the totem pole, and she clearly despised having to kowtow to me.

It's rare that a person who is systematically rude has a change of heart. At our company picnic a couple of months later, Alice sat across from me and made small talk. Moments later, as I walked over to the grill to get a hot dog, she motioned me with her index finger to "come here."

"Oh no," I thought. She was on her turf and was probably going to let me have it. Instead, she asked me to take a walk with her. You can imagine my shock when she broke down and began to cry. Alice confessed that she had been mean to me and asked my forgiveness. She admitted she had taken one look at me and become envious. I accepted her apology, and she never again acted unkind toward me or interfered with my work.

The other undercover agent, another good Mormon guy, ridiculed me for giving her a second chance. How stupid could I be?

Yeah, how stupid *could* I be that I kept trying to do my job in the face of such discouragement from my Bureau cohorts?

CHAPTER 18

BETRAYED WITH A KISS

LIVING A double life is complicated, to say the least. My undercover identity deprived me of the freedom I once enjoyed as a Special Agent. I was used to frequenting— as Barbara Van Driel—places like the corner diner, my favorite upscale hair salon, and, of course, the Federal building. No longer could I just drop in to say hello to my fellow agents or simply meet anywhere for a cup of coffee with a friend. I was now looking over my shoulder all the time.

This was a new way of being for me, and it wasn't all that comfortable.

I could not take the risk of exposing my friends or family to the reality surrounding my false persona. Taking a spin in my undercover sports car might lead to an accidental discovery: anyone could reach innocently into the glove compartment, and voila! A blown cover.

This liability followed me to my front door. Once inside my house, the risks were greater. I had two phone lines. If a visitor noticed the blinking light on my answering machine, the odds were 50/50 that he or she might press the play button without asking first. Again, blown cover.

Yet the thrill of the assignment initially compensated for not being able to socialize as freely. It's really true, one feels like a movie star. My life on the job was filled with intrigue—late night conversations in dark places, meetings with my contact agent in parking garages, excursions to unknown destinations.

Months into the assignment, I began to ponder the reality of my isolation. The initial excitement had worn off. My only lifeline to the Bureau was one person, my contact agent.

This was SA Paul Lofton, a forty-eight-year-old marathon runner with the physique of a twenty-five-year-old. Blue-eyed, with chiseled features, Lofton exuded intensity. Our personalities were initially a good fit, but our goals were ultimately different, as I would soon find out.

From the outset of the assignment, we met at least once a week to discuss the case. We went over strategies and ran through "what if" scenarios. He kept me grounded in reality. I cannot overstate the importance of the relationship between an undercover agent and her contact agent. In my case, I confided in Lofton and placed one-hundred percent trust in him. He provided near-total emotional and psychological support. Lofton was the only person who knew the real me. To everyone else around me all day long, I was someone else. When we met, I could really relax and just be me.

I routinely worked twelve-hour-plus days at my undercover job. My shifts were erratic. Often with short notice, I had to work through the night. I sometimes suffered from sleep deprivation. After work, I came home to an empty house and dictated my "short stories," recounting in minute detail the conversations and events of the day. I was consumed by the job, day and night, which only reinforced my sense of isolation.

More than anything, I lived for the time I spent with Lofton. Our relationship was professional, yet intensely personal because of my total dependency on him. One evening, in March 1990, he called and suggested we get together the following evening for a late dinner and a nice, long talk about the case. I was elated. Our usual meetings were limited to less than an hour, so the idea of having an extended time together felt like a gift.

We went to a bistro around nine o'clock, and I ordered my favorite dish—angel hair pasta with spicy marinara sauce and a side salad, hold the cheese. We talked for hours.

Three hours into our conversation, Lofton's left arm suddenly slithered along the top of the booth, virtually engulfing me in an embrace. Because he was like a brother to me—I guess you could say he was even like the proverbial big brother, since he was fifteen years older than I was—I somewhat dismissed his uninvited affection.

Moments later, tipsy from drinking wine with his meal, Lofton jerked me closer to him and kissed me forcefully on the mouth.

Although my outward demeanor remained steady, inwardly I was panicked, trying to straddle the various implications of the situation. Where was he going with this? Had I once again been duped into believing I had a true friendship? Stunned and caught off guard, I balked, but then let it go, trying to pretend nothing had happened. We continued to talk for a while longer.

"I'm free all night because my wife is out of town," he slobbered.

I could no longer avoid the signs: he had ulterior motives.

"Let's go somewhere for coffee," Lofton suggested.

By this time, it was around midnight.

"It's really getting late, Paul, and I think I'd better go home and get some sleep," I replied.

"Aw, come on," he insisted.

Again, I hesitated to complain too much and risk seeming ungrateful or unpleasant. Besides, Lofton was driving. I wasn't in any position to tell him what to do.

We spent the next two or three hours in an all-night diner, despite my occasional yet persistent requests to be taken home. Snow was falling so hard that, looking out the window toward the parking lot, I could see nothing but white streamers. I felt trapped.

At about three in the morning, Lofton finally agreed to take me home. On the tense ride from downtown Salt

Lake City to my house, I was quiet and introspective. I was sickened by the realization that he had crossed the line. I'd seen this bad movie before. Now all I wanted was to get home.

Lofton didn't say much on the ride either—not until we pulled up in front of my house.

"I want to fuck you," he coarsely uttered.

I bolted out of the car and hurried inside.

Alone in my bed, I never went to sleep. Then, about an hour and a half later, the phone rang.

"Can't I come over?" Lofton cajoled. "I'm all alone."

"No! Why are you calling me?"

"I wanna come back."

He didn't want to take no for an answer. He kept insisting that he should come back. Forget about how *I* felt—he didn't want to pass up a chance for a one-off sexual exploit. After all, that's what it was going to be.

I laid in bed churning over in my mind what had been, what was, and what would be. My heart sank as I admitted to myself that there would be dire consequences for rejecting him.

A few days later, Lofton and I had to meet with the private citizen who'd been cut in on the assignment. It was necessary to have one individual made aware that I was an FBI agent in order to facilitate the undercover operation. It didn't take a genius to notice that Lofton wasn't speaking to me. I can still see him, sitting there with his right ankle resting crosswise over his left knee. He talked almost exclusively to the other person as if I weren't there. I knew in my heart of hearts that our professional relationship was over.

A week or so later, Lofton called me and wanted to meet.

"I'm off the case," he said. "I've pulled myself off. Barrett and I really don't get along."

I couldn't believe my ears. What was I going to do? Who would replace him?

My world collapsed.

CHAPTER 19

FOUL PLAY

JED BAXTER.

That name reverberated in my mind. Baxter had a full head of sandy brown hair, parted on the side. He was 6′2″, slim, with dull, watery, pale-blue eyes. A cradle Mormon, Baxter epitomized the perfect man and the typical FBI agent. He did the minimum required to keep his job and keep the supervisor off his back. He represented the squad mentality: by the numbers and by the book. Forget anything beyond the most basic requirements. He never took time to get to know anyone.

My new contact agent, the equivalent of a potted plant. I knew it was official now: I was being completely and utterly abandoned.

As it turned out, more than two months passed without a meeting with Baxter. For all that time, I was, in essence, cut off completely from the real world, and from my so-called "family," as the Bureau was fond of referring to itself.

Baxter didn't bother to contact me until June. Then he informed me that our meetings would be between five and five-fifteen, on his way home from work. We met at a fast food restaurant just outside of Salt Lake City no more frequently than once a month. He wouldn't even sit down. He would drink his glass of milk, pick up my dictated reports, and leave. No moral support, no conversation—no nothing.

Sleep deprivation started taking a toll on me. My work schedule varied so wildly that, even though I was supposed to work days, many times the boss asked me to work all night. So it was difficult to constantly adjust my sleep cycle from night to day. On top of that problem, I dedicated hours to writing reports pertaining to my assignment.

I remember once, in the middle of the night, sitting at my desk, I actually thought a vehicle was heading toward me. But a moment later, I snapped out of it only to realize nothing was there. I was hallucinating from sleep deprivation.

Exacerbating my isolation had been the emotional blowback from the devastating news, fifteen months earlier, of the sudden death of the man I had hoped to marry.

Psychologically, I could no longer endure the extreme isolation. I drove home during the day on August 14, 1990, called Dr. Malcolm Streeter, the psychologist at Quantico, and asked for help. I told him I wanted off the case. The situation was intolerable, the behavior of my contact agents was unspeakably cruel, and my life was unbearable.

It's difficult to explain how I felt maintaining two identities. My fake persona, created by Lofton and me, was a widow from back east. And now, in real life, I felt like I had been widowed. I was concerned to let the Bureau know how upset I was by my personal loss. You know, the case had to go on, no matter what.

"Asking for help" turned out to be more like "asking for trouble."

CHAPTER 20

SELF-INDICTMENT

IN JUNE, I first met Dr. Malcolm Streeter in person in Salt Lake City when he had come from Quantico to administer some psychological tests and conduct interviews with the undercover agents. This was routine for the Bureau, part of their responsibility. Gleaning from its history, the Bureau officially recognized the obligation to nurture and support employees, especially when they worked undercover. Official position aside, the reality was something far less.

I warned Dr. Streeter that I was under duress and that my contact agent, Baxter, was refusing to meet with me. Dr. Streeter promised me he would speak to my supervisor and caution him about the need for Baxter to be proactive and available.

Unfortunately, Dr. Streeter's intervention on my behalf in June went unheeded.

After I had placed the phone call in August to Dr. Streeter, my supervisor, John Barrett, called me and set up an appointment for us to meet at the Village Inn in midtown Salt Lake City the next day at noon. At the restaurant, I sat nervously with Barrett and attempted to explain why I had called Dr. Streeter and why I wanted to be removed from the undercover assignment.

Even though my contact agents had let me down, I felt terrible that I could no longer function effectively in the position. I blamed myself for not being superhuman enough to survive without support.

Although respectful, Barrett seemed annoyed and concerned more about himself and the ramifications of my calling a halt to the assignment. It would reflect negatively on him. He had obviously failed to reprimand Baxter. Nothing had changed from the time Dr. Streeter interviewed me until then—in more than two months.

Dissatisfied with my explanation, Barrett pried into my emotional and psychological states of being, wondering if there was something—anything—that I was not telling him.

Grappling for words, I admitted I was confused about my feelings for someone with whom I had contact on the assignment. Big mistake. Barrett latched on to that statement and wouldn't let go. The more I tried to explain what I meant, the deeper the hole I dug.

Barrett had found a way to justify the inadequacies of his agent. He acted like I had fallen in love with the "enemy," and, even though he was sweating it out, he'd found a scapegoat for my behavior.

"Go home, stay there, and wait for a telephone call," he instructed me.

In retrospect, I had done nothing wrong. It was just that one of the targets, a dark-haired, slim man, who reminded me of my deceased friend, had gone out of his way to be kind to me. We did no more than take walks near a waterfall, share a soda together, and enjoy late-night talks. All of these activities were part of my undercover assignment, my way of assessing targets. More to the point, Barrett and I had, early on, discussed the global idea of interacting with people on such an intimate level so as to facilitate a "viable relationship" beneficial to the U.S. government.

It was difficult for Barrett to understand or believe I was telling the truth. It wasn't as if I'd had an affair with a target. The subtlety of my explanation eluded him. I read his cold demeanor as meaning, "You have no idea how much trouble you're in."

CHAPTER 21

UNDER THE SPYGLASS

WITHIN DAYS, I was put on a plane and flown to Quantico for many rounds of interviews and psychological testing. Forbidden to leave the premises during my two-week stay, I was "imprisoned" there, for all practical purposes, and uncertain about my future. After all, the Bureau wasn't sure what was really going on with me, and it needed to make sure I had not compromised the operation.

"For your own good, you can't leave Quantico," Dr. Streeter advised.

One of the psychological exams consisted of approximately 600-700 questions, true or false. I remember several of them because of their poignancy or ridiculousness:

"There is something that has happened in my life that I know I will never get over."

"Voices tell me what to do."

"Ministering spirits direct my thoughts and actions."

I chose "false" as my answer to all the above. The scary two were correct: I'd never heard voices nor had spirits tell me what to think or do. But in my heart of hearts, I was afraid to answer "true" to the first statement, even though I knew I would never get over the death of my dear friend.

While you're taking these tests and being interviewed, you've already learned through experience that it's impossible to be totally candid with the Bureau. In defense of the testing process, the questions were designed to identify agents who had "gone off the reservation." Following the extensive testing, Dr. Streeter informed me that, both back in June and presently, my psychological health fell within the normal range.

Dr. Streeter discussed the results with me. He said my profiling brought out two pronounced characteristics: the need to belong and my fierce independence. He summed up the latter with this quip: "Buy yourself a leather coat and spray paint 'Lone Wolf' on the back."

He told me the test was double-blind, designed to identify people who tried to appear other than they are. I knew there was nothing the matter with me. My feelings and reactions were legitimate and justified, considering what both contact agents had done. These issues and others we discussed at length.

I spoke with one agent who was also there being "retooled." He had gone through a terrible personal and professional crisis as a result of his more than two-year undercover assignment in rural Kentucky. Every day, he had to make believe he was this sheriff's buddy while fearing the redneck would discover his true identity. He was forced to live apart from his family in order to maintain his undercover role. Eventually, his wife left him.

My heart went out to my colleague as he confided in me that he did not feel he could ever work again as an agent. He had gone through the same thing I had: his contact agent had abandoned him.

Thankfully, Dr. Streeter supported me throughout this process. I'd passed through the narrow gate of scrutiny by the "family." Once again, I was back in their good graces.

CHAPTER 22

EMANCIPATION PROCLAMATION

I'VE NEVER seen myself as a quitter. The closest I'd ever come was stopping college in my early 20s and taking a couple of years to reconsider my educational goals. Since the winter of '79, I'd been on a trajectory toward a career in law enforcement. I'd never looked back.

Being in the Bureau felt like an arranged marriage. I took the oath for life, so any consideration to leave became more like considering a divorce than a resignation. Percolating in my mind since April 1989 was the decision I'd made not to resign from the FBI in the spring of 1988. Based on these persistent thoughts, October 6, 1990, I designated as my D-Day—the day I would finally leave.

I carried hidden remorse over not leaving in April 1988, but I had some ambivalence because there was no clear path for me after the Bureau, now that the love of my life was gone.

I dwelled on several thoughts that converged at this point in my life. The incidents of abuse in the Bureau, my unresolved anger at myself for changing my mind in 1988 and staying, and my inability to any longer identify with the goals, as unclear as they were, of the Bureau.

Working in CI was problematic because no tangible results materialized. It felt like a series of one-night stands, minus the sex. I dreaded the fact that a lifetime spent in this work would result in an empty portfolio—reams of paper stacked in a classified vault.

It was pure anguish one day when I had the unfortunate experience to actually read one of my dictated reports from the undercover assignment I had been on. The dictation was submitted to the typing pool by Lofton. One secretary, in particular, made it her "life's work" to type my reports. The sentences trailed off into irrationality at the point at which the secretary couldn't understand what I was trying to say in my dictation. Completely useless.

No attempt had been made to correct these gross inaccuracies. When I asked Lofton about this problem, he laughed: "Barbara, no one ever read your reports. Twenty or thirty copies were made, and they just went in the files."

Infuriated, I said to myself, "None of my hard work ever mattered."

Lofton added, "You know, when you'd write your reports, agents would come up to me and laugh. They sounded like fiction."

I jumped in—"Are you trying to say I made things up?"

"Well, you often had quotes, and the stories seemed phantasmal."

"Paul, that's what was said, and I was able to quote people verbatim from memory."

—

I left my resignation statement with SAC George Taylor's secretary (Taylor had replaced Thompson several months earlier). The next thing I knew I was sitting in Taylor's office.

"I'm not accepting your resignation," he stated bluntly, and tore my letter of resignation in two. He wanted to know what my plans were.

"I have no plans," I said honestly. "I'm just leaving." I must have come across as listless and defeated.

"I'm going to keep you on criminal work and see to it that you become a more well-rounded agent. You need to get away from CI investigations."

During this conversation, I sensed a true feeling of support and concern from Taylor. Although his counsel made sense on one hand, working Criminal Matters held no appeal for me. But what I had loved to do had become unbearable. I was in a quandary.

"My door is always open to you," he added. "Come by anytime you need to talk."

That was an honor. He let me know that he had the highest respect for me.

Some of the agents in the office cautioned me, "George Taylor eats agents, he'll destroy your career." Regardless of what they said, because I knew they were jealous and hateful, I defended Taylor. Their comments meant nothing to me; I was confident that he was genuine.

CHAPTER 23

THE BRIBE

AS MY favorite uncle, Henry, often said, "A man convinced against his will is of the same opinion still." Words that ran through my mind as I considered the quandary I found myself in. So many "wills" in play: Lofton, Baxter, Barrett, Taylor. Me.

I resigned myself to remain in the Bureau for the time being, but I continued to wrestle with ambivalence. Unfortunately, my nefarious contact agents, Paul Lofton and Jed Baxter, emerged unscathed from their unprofessional and unethical behaviors. In the office with them now, I noticed they were oblivious and in denial with respect to the serious harm they had caused me.

With what I took as genuine concern for my well-being, SAC Taylor kept our conversation going about the following: whether I should lodge formal EEO complaints against Lofton and Baxter, remain in the Salt Lake City Division (under his tutelage) and work Criminal Matters, or request a transfer. These issues were intertwined.

So much so that the decision regarding the EEO complaints eventually resulted in an extraordinary offer from FBI Headquarters: the opportunity to choose any division in the country for an immediate transfer.

This extravagant offer mysteriously coincided with tremors felt throughout FBI Headquarters when those in authority were informed that I might be filing formal complaints based on the misconduct of two agents. Knowing how unorthodox it was to receive this kind of preferential treatment, I thought the gesture was only to placate me, perhaps with the hope that all the ugly incidents would be forgotten.

I was blown away that day Taylor relayed the unbelievable offer. It's nearly impossible to explain how unorthodox it is for an agent to jump any OP list. For example, an agent whose OP was San Diego might have to wait fifteen years or more to get there. And here it was that I was being offered the chance to, in essence, jump the line to number one on *any* division list. Unreal.

I knew this offer was loaded. Not only was I uncertain what office would be best, but I also knew the ramifications were potentially ugly. My fellow agents would find out I had jumped the list and label me a prima donna, or worse (the unusual access I enjoyed to the SAC had already generated resentment and paranoia). My reputation was at stake. Wherever I chose to go, people would assume I was being paid off—either to keep my mouth shut or for "services rendered."

So, I was between a rock and a hard place: take a transfer to my dream division, or file the EEO complaints.

During this time of consideration, I was confronted one day by my ASAC.

"If you proceed against these guys, you'll be sorry," he sneered as he rhythmically slapped a cardboard tube against his palm. In typical Bureau fashion, unbeknownst to Taylor, this guy was threatening me, and the message was loud and clear. And I got it.

What exactly would happen to me? I had no idea. But I was smart enough to know that this ASAC, with his stinky cigar breath and frowny mustache, wasn't what you'd call a "nice guy." He could taste the SAC's position, his next step up, and no one was going to damage his chances. No one. If I had succeeded in bringing down Lofton and Baxter, their downfall would have underscored his negligence. And he wasn't going to let that happen—not on his watch.

In any case, I got the message. He never spoke to me again. Such was the esprit de corps on which the Bureau prided itself.

———

After much soul-searching, and against the advice of my SAC, I dismissed the idea of filing the EEO complaints. I remember Taylor saying, "You hold the future of their careers in your hands." In my mind, although they had done wrong, they were family men. Not only would they have been punished, but also their families would have been victims of their indiscretions and negligence. Once again, I put the well-being of others and the Bureau ahead of my own.

The offer was still on the table to go anywhere I wanted to go. I made phone calls, talked to a lot of agents, and finally decided on Dallas. In fact, someone on the CI squad in Dallas called me and said, "We can't wait until you get here. You're going to be our number-one Soviet expert."

Oh, great. I wouldn't have described myself as any kind of expert. Furthermore, it was flattering, but was it the best direction to take? And the word on the street was the SAC in Dallas was not someone I wanted to work under.

Which way to turn, which way to go? I had made my choice, but, in reality, there were no good choices in front of me. Not in the Bureau, anyway.

CHAPTER 24

TOP GUN

CAN YOU picture a Tom-Cruise prototype strutting around the squad room, his Smith & Wesson 10mm shoved into the back waistband of his jeans? Would Cruise prop his feet on his desk and spit in the nearby trashcan? SA Gunner Smith, Salt Lake City's answer to *Top Gun*, fit this description perfectly, except he was married, had three children, and kept a mistress. He was movie-star material—minus the good looks—waiting to be discovered.

SAC Taylor put me on the squad with this guy, and, lucky me, I got to work as his understudy. For Smith, becoming an FBI agent was a demotion. A former Air Force pilot, nothing could be as exciting as flying those planes, breaking the sound barrier, spinning through space.

Smith made do with this mundane job, bleeding it for as much drama as possible.

One time, he was setting up a scenario for catching a bank robber. Every other Friday, a bank robbery had occurred in a certain area of town, so the Bureau had been called in to preempt another incident. We were putting into place our surveillance team with perimeter people, someone in the bank, and a "point" man (would-be sniper).

Smith selected a neophyte agent for the sniper post and put on quite a show for us.

"You! Take him out!" he dramatically exhorted. "And if you see anything—anything at all—don't hesitate! Take him down!"

Slowly, the neophyte got "in the zone." He was what you would call the reluctant sniper, but Smith egged him on until the newbie played along and joined in the staged frenzy.

The irony here was the bank robber never showed up and was later arrested single-handedly by a plain-clothes detective. Immediately upon being stopped, the robber confessed that he had robbed the banks in order to feed his family. He didn't even have a deadly weapon; it was a toy gun. This uneventful conclusion to the bank-robbery spree slowly made the rounds to the bemusement of everyone except "Top Gun."

Even during a routine arrest involving a subject without a weapon, he allowed his testosterone level to run rampant and dictate over-the-top antics. One day, we surrounded a UFAP as he drove his dilapidated car up to the trailer park mailboxes. Leaping out of three Bureau cars, clad in bulletproof vests, we rushed forward in pairs and surrounded the dented, blue two-door sedan.

"FBI! You're under arrest!" Smith screamed, adding on second thought, "Are you Little Eagle Feather?"

"Nah," the guy mumbled.

"Let me see your ankle!" Smith was escalating. He lifted up the left cuff of the guy's jeans, and pointed out to us his identifying tattoo. "You fucking liar! You son of a bitch! You are him! Now get out of the car!"

I was afraid Smith was going to shoot him.

There were six of us on the arrest team. The Native American was so inebriated he could barely lift himself out of his car.

Another agent and I went to the passenger side of the car and helped an elderly man get out. He obviously had no idea what was going on. We quietly explained he wasn't in any trouble. We could still hear "Top Gun" hollering at the drunk driver.

Finally, Smith and I got back in the Bureau car, and the subject, along with his passenger, was transported to the Marshall's office. During my ride back to the office with "Top Gun," I pointedly asked him, "Do we have to defame someone in order to arrest him?" No answer.

I had the uneasy feeling that his extreme temper was Smith's way of looking for a fight. He was heading for a shoot-out, and I determined I wasn't going along on the next ride.

So much for working "sexy" criminal cases.

CHAPTER 25

DARK DAYS AT QUANTICO

GLOOMY CLOUDS filled the damp winter skies that hung over Quantico one early January morning in 1991. Against the advice of SAC George Taylor, I decided to go to our training facility to work as a counselor for new agents. Taylor had warned me not to get involved with "that world," but I thought I could be a positive role model. Besides, I needed something to do while I waited for transfer orders to Dallas.

One clown, my co-counselor-to-be for the new class, called me in Salt Lake City before I left. After a few perfunctory niceties, he quipped, "Hey! Are we going to be taking a shower together naked?"

"Do you have a Buddha belly?" I retorted. That shut him up.

With slight misgivings, I arrived at Quantico. My space for the next sixteen weeks would be the counselors' office, plus a pleasant dorm room in the newest wing of the facility. I met lots of nice agents. My luck—the one guy I'd been paired with as my co-counselor was a jerk.

The second week, we headed for Bear Mountain, NY. It was a tactical driving school set up by the Bureau at a closed airport. Each group had to be there two and a half days, so I went along with half of the new agents in my class.

The first day, we spent a couple of hours in a class-room where one of the two agents assigned to the school instructed agents in special driving techniques. Out on the runway, cars were parked. Mutt and Jeff, the two main instructors, feigned stereotypical homosexual affects, rocked the cars until they nearly tipped over, and basically acted like two juvenile delinquents.

The new agents with me didn't think the pair was funny, especially when Jeff asked one young female, "When's the last time you had an orgasm?"

Moments later, Mutt came around behind me and shoved each of his hands into the front pockets of my trousers. He poked his fingers down deep, trying to get a rise out of me. I pushed him off.

In the evenings, it was clear these guys had a drink-ing problem. They boozed it up with some of the new agents, despite Bureau protocol to the contrary.

On the last morning, Mutt ended his closing pre-sentation by drawing a picture on the board of a man's dangling testicles to illustrate the punch-line of a vulgar joke. No one laughed.

After this warm-up act, he passed out evaluation forms to the class and winked. Several of the women in the class later confided in me that they were mortified by the behavior of the two clowns.

The next day, back at Quantico, I bumped into Dr. Malcolm Streeter in the "Boardroom" (Quantico's in-house restaurant and bar). I mentioned what had happened up at Bear Mountain. He said he understood we were talking off the record. My advice: someone needed to investigate the driving school because it was a lawsuit waiting to happen. I worried about the risk the Bureau was taking by exposing new agents to sexual harassment.

By the next day, I was called in by some big muckety-muck in charge of new agents. He wanted a formal report. I resisted, remembering the maxim, "shoot the messenger."

Within a couple of days, Mutt and Jeff showed up at Quantico. When I passed them in the hall, they were coming out of the Boardroom. They grinned in a mocking way. Their mannerism communicated, "No one can touch us."

The Bureau ordered one of the new female agents in my class to write a report about what had happened to her at Bear Mountain, but she didn't want to. In fact, I went to see her and found her crying over the whole mess. She had enough savvy to recognize this move would not be good for her career. She would begin her life in the Bureau already labeled as a whistleblower.

I suspected that Mutt and Jeff had good reason to know they wouldn't get in trouble. They knew how to keep book.

CHAPTER 26

RESIGNATION REDUX

THE FALL-OUT following my confidential suggestion to Dr. Streeter that someone investigate the unprofessional conduct of the two bozos who ran the driving school at Bear Mountain had the typical consequences when it came to the Bureau and the truth.

"You've made people uncomfortable," one supervisor told me. "You're willing to tell the truth, and I respect you for it, but you'll have to leave Quantico."

Once again, I'd found myself in a predicament. I became absolutely convinced that a person like me did not belong in the Bureau. The fidelity and integrity in "FBI" were gone.

I packed my bags and said the few goodbyes I was permitted. My instructions had been succinct: you are not to speak to the new agents. Damage control.

As Dr. Streeter drove me to Dulles Airport, I no longer cared to speak with him. I doubted his sincerity for the first time: he had denied ever revealing my confidence, but somehow that circumspect, private conversation went like wildfire up the chain of command at Quantico. And he had no reasonable explanation for the pass given to the clowns.

He reiterated that he had defended me in front of the Quantico brass.

"They don't understand you. They can't understand a person with your sense of integrity."

This was supposed to comfort me somehow.

"Why are you so quiet?" he asked.

"I'm leaving."

"Please, promise me you won't resign from the Bureau."

"I'm going back to Utah and resigning."

He begged me over and over to reconsider. I was resolute—no more indecision.

—

Back at Salt Lake City, I relayed to SAC Taylor what had happened at Quantico.

"I told you not to go," he admonished.

"I know, but I wanted to help the new agents."

"Well, this wouldn't have happened if you had just stayed here in Salt Lake City."

"You're right."

"So now what?"

"I really want to leave—I've made up my mind."

This time around Taylor was supportive. He could see my anguish, and he felt I must follow my own instincts. He wouldn't stand in my way.

I submitted my thirty-day notice on April 3, 1991.

The next couple of weeks I fielded a few pleas of "Don't go! Don't go!" from several people in the office. One man even went so far as to write a long letter pleading with me to stay.

Although I was touched by their sincerity, it wasn't going to happen. This time there would be no turning back.

CHAPTER 27

LAST DETAIL

WITH HIS hair sprayed coiffure and self-conscious attention to style, SA L. Woodman Cleaves looked more like Oscar Wilde than a real FBI agent. I couldn't imagine how this guy ever made it through Quantico—I just couldn't picture him breaking a sweat.

When he walked, he wiggled his heinie, feet turned out slightly, with a middle-aged, pooched belly leading the way. As Cleaves conducted my exit interview, the pursuit began; he seemed determined to get me to say something derogatory about the Bureau. With his feigned attitude of concern, he baited me.

"What's your real reason for leaving the Bureau?" he chortled.

"I'm leaving for personal reasons."

"What's your *real* reason for leaving the Bureau?"

"I'm leaving for personal reasons."

He pointed at me with his pen, which he held like a cigarette. Then he turned his hand over, palm up, and made figure eights in the air. Total affect.

Again, he asked: "What is your *real reason* for leaving the Bureau?"

I repeated my mantra: "I'm leaving for personal reasons."

The truth was far too complex and painful to explain; besides, ultimately, reasons were irrelevant.

Cleaves showed me the form on which he could check "eligible" or "not eligible" for rehire. I paid close attention as he checked the "eligible" for rehire box. It was my intention to leave the Bureau in good standing. I refused to leave with any black marks on my record.

Following my exit interview with SA Cleaves, I quietly picked up my few belongings and took one last look at my desk and around the squad room. No one spoke to me.

What was I leaving? A lot, for sure—and not so much. My dream—and a terrible nightmare.

That last Friday as I departed the Federal building, I silently rode the elevator down to the lobby. The large glass double-doors loomed before me. Passing through them, I took a deep breath and contemplated for a moment what my new life might look like. I was determined to not only survive but to flourish. There *would be* "life after the Bureau" for me. Wounded, yes—defeated, never.

I looked up: it was a blue-sky day.

EPILOGUE

ONE WEEK after leaving the Bureau, I had occasion to return to the Federal building in order to take care of some "housekeeping." As I approached the bank of elevators in the lobby, I noticed one of the agents from my former squad exiting. He looked right through me as we passed by each other. I no longer existed.

That may have been the case as far as the Bureau was concerned, but I was excited about the next chapter of my life, and I wasn't looking for any validation from my former associates. My decision to leave the Bureau, albeit fraught with ambiguities, was done freely, and as much as it hurt to leave the "family," I knew it was the only way for me to live my convictions without compromise. Eight-plus years of trying to conform to the system was enough.

My message now, as then, is this: each person must live their life on their own terms and have the courage to face the consequences of their choices. Discomfort doesn't matter. What others think doesn't matter. What matters is living an ethical life: with fidelity, with bravery, with integrity.

ABOUT THE AUTHOR

Barbara Van Driel was a Special Agent in the FBI from February 1983 to May 1991. She worked primarily in the area of Counterintelligence, electing to study the Russian language in order to focus on investigative matters pertaining to the former Soviet Union. Subsequent to her time with the Bureau, she traveled extensively to Russia and Ukraine where she enjoyed the various peoples and cultures of that vast region.

After a somewhat protracted, self-directed sabbatical of sorts, Barbara embarked on a ten-year career in the medical field: managing a medical practice; working in critical care in a hospital setting; and caring for the chronically and critically ill in their homes. This work was immensely fulfilling, allowing her to express her ethic of care and compassion for others.

Over the past ten years, Barbara has become an entrepreneur and has returned to studying classical piano. She travels widely, both domestically and overseas, and splits her time between San Diego, Chicago, Palm Springs, and rural Wyoming.

CPSIA information can be obtained
at www.ICGtesting.com
Printed in the USA
FSHW01n0608041018
52749FS